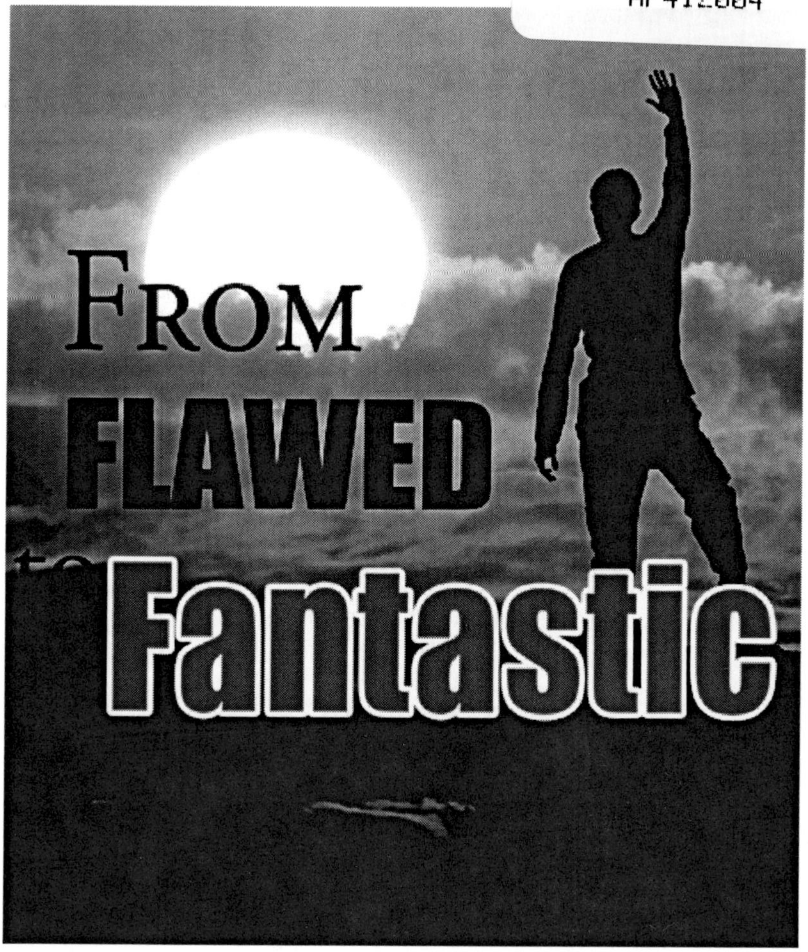
FROM
FLAWED
to
Fantastic

HOW I TURNED MY DISABILITY INTO AN A$$ET

—FANTASTIC FRANK

 www.FantasticFrankJohnson.com

Editing by Jami Lynn Sands.

DEDICATION

To Michael Blum

My best friend of 25 years, Michael Blum, passed away during the writing of this book. I mentored Michael, and he inspired me. Like most good friends, we did not always see eye to eye on everything. However, that did not get in the way of the very deep bond that our friendship was based on.

This book is for all of the other Michaels out there.

ACKNOWLEDGMENTS

Frank Gasiorowski

Without Frank Gasiorowski, this book would not exist. He has been my mentor for years. From the beginning, he saw something special in me, that I did not see in myself. It was Frank's loving influence, his belief in me, and his firm yet flexible direction, that has made this book possible.

He not only inspired me, but also coached me along the way to give the talks on which this book is based. Giving those talks propelled me forward, and gave me clarity that I have the ability to inspire and motivate others.

In addition to being my mentor on a professional level, he is my friend. He knows me better than anyone else, except God.

Marvelous Michele Camacho

Michele started working with me on this book as a transcriptionist for my talks, and from that evolved into my assistant and my friend. She knows me so well, that she anticipates my words and knows what I am going to say before I speak. She helps me express my feelings in a succinct written form. When we were working on the Branding Chapter, I branded her "Marvelous Michele" because it fits her so well.

Tracy Repchuk

Tracy came into play when the manuscript was already prepared. In a flash, she saved this book from being self-published with a mediocre cover, and probably read by no one. It was Tracy who made the personal connection with Justin Sachs, enabling Motivation Press to publish this book. With great expertise in understanding the nuances of designing the right cover for the right niche, she guided the cover design to ensure it is the image it should be.

Justin Sachs

Justin has overwhelmed me with his incredible professionalism, personal care, and lighting fast responses day and night. He started our relationship by calling me directly, giving me freedom to discuss all questions, ensuring I understood the process fully. He personally responded to all communications regarding every aspect of designing this book.

From our first phone call, I had the emotional realization that something "real" was going to happen with this book, after years of wandering in development. Motivations Press's capacity for global marketing and distribution raises my ability to touch others with my message to a whole other stratosphere. This may well be the springboard that makes my "motivation" to inspire millions a reality.

Anthony Robbins

Anthony Robbins helped to make me aware of how to help other people. He sparked the passion in me to grow into becoming Fantastic Frank.

Everyone Else

I am of course aware that I am leaving people out, like my family, including my ex-wife, and all the people in my life who support me or whom I've impacted. There are also those who have helped me grow and change. If you have impacted my life in any way, and you don't see your name here, please know that I am thinking about you. For the sake of brevity, I have to end this section. It would take a book in itself to fully acknowledge everyone else.

TESTIMONIALS

Fantastic Frank, Amazing Frank, Energizing Frank would all be proper descriptions for this special man. 'Fantastic Frank' says it best to describe this unique individual with a unique story. You will read his special story and then learn lessons of inspiration, motivation and most of all perseverance. Frank has spent years learning optimal thinking and now shares his knowledge to push you and lock out any and all excuses you may be tempted to use. If you are facing any of life's challenges or even think you are, this book is a must for your night stand!

—Doug Evans, Success and Abundance Coach
www.discoveryourmissingpower.com

What's holding you back from achieving success in your field? Chances are the obstacles standing in your way are the ones you've created in your own mind.

Fantastic Frank is one of the most amazing people I've ever met! Fantastic Frank has a disability, which he refers to as being *Differently-Abled*.

Fantastic Frank is right; he is *Differently-Abled*. He has the *Ability* to make us look at ourselves and say, "If Fantastic Frank can do it, if he can achieve his goals and dreams, so can I."

Fantastic Frank is an inspiration to me. He takes away all our excuses. He is an example of what can be accomplished when we follow our dreams.

—Michael Chapple, President & CEO E.D.C.
Eagle Distributing Company, Inc.
www.homefiresafety.com

Handwritten Letter from James Malinchak, "America's Achievement Coach," May, 2011

Hi "Fantastic" Frank –

You are such an inspirational person and I am very grateful to have met you.

—James Malinchak,
Featured on ABC's "The Secret Millionaire"

You inspired our people and provided the perfect inspirational message for our annual convention! In addition to your unbelievable attitude of thanks and grace, you exhibited a CANI-ing determination! Our people have overwhelmed us with comments of how perfect you were for our company! On a personal level, you stirred my soul and made me ask myself, "what excuses do I have that prohibit me from achieving the purpose God has for me?". Thank you for allowing God to use you to stir my spirit. I wish you all the best in your pursuit of being the voice for empowering people! You have my heart!

—Chris Roberts,President
Global Health and Safety Companies

Who would have thought so much would come from just a phone call to come out to dinner.

I have heard many speakers over the years, including President Reagan, and you were the most inspirational of them all.

You are going on from here to achieve all your dreams.

—Jerry Larrabee

You truly are Fantastic!! I'll never forget the blessing of having you at my program. I know that you are destined for tremendous and fantastic things in your future.

Blessed will be all of the people to have a privilege to meet you as I am. Thank you for your words of wisdom and encouragement. In a very short time you have made a difference in my life.

—Dan Gallant

To persevere and overcome the personal tragedy you suffered from fire is a testament to the strength of the human spirit when you turn it over to God to find happiness and success. God Bless You!

—Fred and Cathy Oller

God Bless you and your family. I am a firefighter. EMT-B. You are an inspiration. You brought a tear to my eyes. I got very emotional. Thank you – Keep on keeping on. God Bless you,

—Vance Howeton

My heart was touched by your story. I think that what you do is amazing, and I think you should share your story with everyone. Thank you so much. I only wish the best for you.

—Brittney Roberson

You are a true inspiration and a genuine person. We enjoyed hearing your speech and talking with you later. Thank you for sharing your story with us and reminding us why we are in the fire education and safety business.

—Sincerely, Michele and Jeff Day

FOREWORD

Let me tell you about a unique individual. His name is Frank R. Johnson.

I first heard Frank on a motivational teleconference call. This guy had a way of cutting through everyone else to ask his questions at the end of the call. At first, I was taken aback as he seemed to force his way into the mix of callers. After knowing Frank R. Johnson, I could see that that was his way and one of his powers.

I was presenting a teleconference on "Branding" and I asked everyone to come up with their brand and a nickname to present that brand. Frank came on at the end of the workshop and enthusiastically shouted out, I'm "Fantastic Frank."

Why is Frank R. Johnson so fantastic? I was to learn during the years that I have known him that he is more than fantastic; he is actually "Extraordinarily-Fantastic."

Frank's life was held on a thread after being trapped in fire over 30 years ago. He was diagnosed with a Traumatic Brain Injury (TBI). After recovering from a coma and years of rehabilitation he receives therapy even today. Don't let this fool you in thinking that his mind is slow. That is so far from the truth. Fantastic Frank is one of the most prolific writers that I have ever coached. Frank also teaches motivation to TBI clients at PRALID and other mental health centers in Rochester, NY.

Once you meet Fantastic Frank you will never forget him. His enthusiasm and shear motivational character is exhilarating and magnetic. While walking down a street in downtown

Baltimore with him people would gravitate towards Fantastic Frank. People are drawn toward this positive person and want to be around him.

This is the first book written by Fantastic Frank and the pre-launch reports from reviewers are nothing short of fantastic. Is a disability a curse or a gift? You tell me after you read this motivational training workshop. I realized that we (everyone) have a disability and that disability can be turned into a gift. This book gives us the tools to make our life truly "FANTASTIC" if we only take the steps that "Fantastic Frank" is bringing to our attention.

—by Frank Gasiorowski,
90-Day Goals Coach

TABLE OF CONTENTS

Introduction: How to Use This Book

Thank you for taking your valuable time to read this book. I am honored and blessed that you are coming into my life in this way. Even though we may not meet in person, I feel a personal connection with everyone who reads this book.

The goal of this book is to help to enlighten you, give you wisdom, and possibly entertain you. One of my missions in life is to serve others. I want to be an inspiration to each one of you and to assist each of you in maximizing your life, by giving love in every moment.

First of all, you are not reading this book by accident. Everything happens for a reason. What drew you to this book? Are you differently-abled (my term for "disabled")? Are you trying to help someone? Are you looking for help or just general knowledge? Are you in a crisis?

How you use this book depends on what drew you to it. You can benefit simply by reading it for general knowledge. If you want to take things a step further, and make changes in your life, then there are Action Steps at the end of each chapter to make the process personally yours.

I can't know exactly what a person is going through in their life. If you have to change some of these action steps, if you have to reframe them, or write something entirely different down, please do so. You will know what resonates with your energy and what doesn't.

It is important that you write these things down, because there is energy associated with writing, which will allow you to make progress. Perhaps you should have a specially designated notebook or journal. If you cannot express your thoughts through writing, then use a computer or have someone else write things down for you.

The order of the topics in this book follows the way that I went through a process. It starts out with the story of what happened to me, of how I became differently-abled and turned that into an asset. From there it moves into how I converted these problems into challenges and then into opportunities. I learned how to use my reticular activating system, or "Scooby Ears and Eyes". I discovered hidden talents and became branded as Fantastic Frank. Along the way, I discovered that words have energy. By not using the word "depression", I improved my chances of happiness. I found out about goal setting and achieving. Then came making distinctions, mentoring, and CANI-ing (making Consistent And Never-ending Improvements).

Your process may happen in a different order; so if you are reading a Chapter, which does not resonate with you, re-examine what drew you to this book and go to another chapter.

I would be honored to hear about how you were affected by this book, if you would like to share your story with me. I value your privacy and will not share your specific personal information. You can write to me at Frank@FantasticFrankJohnson.com

For a Quick Start

- Review the Table of Contents.
- Go to the chapter you are most attracted to.
- Read the Action Steps at the end of each chapter.
- Read the Chapter
- Act on the Action Steps

Chapter One

Disability: A Curse or a Gift from God?

The Fantastic Frank Story

This chapter is my story, and it is your story, too. That is because we all have something, which we allow to keep us from maximizing our happiness. You may not have something that meets the definition of a "disability" per the American Disability Act (ADA), but perhaps you allow yourself to be limited by your beliefs, your physical appearance, your economic status, your ethnicity, your fear of being hurt, your self-doubt, something you have not forgiven, or countless other things which feel like a curse.

As you read this chapter, I invite you to 'feel' deeper into things in your life that have felt like curses, and to celebrate the ones that you have grown beyond. I invite you to strive to see the gifts in your life by stepping out of the trauma and drama of life and change your perspective.

My name is Fantastic Frank. I've been differently-abled for over 30 years, with a Traumatic Brain Injury (TBI). The TBI resulted from carbon monoxide poisoning, which caused a lack of oxygen to my brain when I was trapped in a fire. I use the term "differently-abled" instead of "disabled" because it is empowering, and suggests a gift.

Part of telling my story is to give a somewhat chronological accounting of my life. There are also milestones which deeply affected me, such as my own 'Conversation with God', writing a song called "Today's Not Going to be Like Yesterday", and attending Tony Robbins events. I will tell you what I felt were 'curses' and the 'gifts' that came from them. I will also tell you how you can make this shift in your own life. At the end of this chapter are "Action Steps" which you can take to get started on implementing these concepts in your own life.

I never thought I was going to become differently-abled. When I got a TBI, at first I thought that it was because I was cursed. At that time, I did not understand why this was happening to me, until I started looking at the situation in a different light. I don't know how I made this shift, but now I look at my being differently-abled as a blessing, not as a curse. The glass is neither half empty nor half full.

Many people think that God curses them. I feel that God doesn't curse anyone, and that God is here for everyone. You might think that God cursed me, but I feel He did not. This understanding took years, and I am now closer in touch with my Creator than I was before having a TBI.

People have had what is commonly referred to as a 'NDE' or Near Death Experience. This is when they have technically died and come back. They have said that our 'understanding' of God is completely different than who He really is.

I would recommend you read the series of books, "Conversations with God", by Neale Donald Walsch, because it will change your perspective of who God is. Years after getting a TBI, I had what I call my own "Conversation with God before I was born". It came as a dream, and it appeared to have happened before I was born. In this conversation, I agreed to become differently-abled, so that I can fulfill a purpose that I believe God asked of me, which is to help others.

Having this dream, or 'conversation', completely changed my outlook. Now I can see that having a TBI is a necessary part of my destiny, and I am not surprised by whatever I have to go through. Sometimes I wish experiencing it wasn't necessary, but I believe I signed on for this before I was born. The dream of this conversation just reinforced what I felt in my heart. I love helping people, and they can feel my sincerity.

I am very passionate about helping other people who have a TBI, and their friends and families, but I won't stop there. I also want to help anyone who is in crisis, or who wants to maximize their happiness. That is why this book is for everyone.

Part of recovering from a crisis is a concept called 'perspective'. This relates to what you are able to see and understand about a situation. If you are currently in a crisis, you may be unable to step back and observe the crisis and view the entire process. Your perspective is limited. All you can see is what is in front of you.

You will need help to step back and look at a broader view, and see that everything goes through the same cycle. Things happen, you suffer, and you get over it. You ask yourself why you put up with a challenge, and why you put yourself through something for years. Eventually, you are able to see the blessings, because your perspective has changed.

The part of my story that has helped me to view this "curse" as a blessing from God, is that becoming "disabled" was foreshadowed years before the accident, in the form of a song I wrote for the United Way called "Today's Not Gonna Be Like Yesterday©." I wrote the following words, and a friend put it to music. A three -minute United Way video using this song has also been posted on YouTube.

Today's Not Gonna to be Like Yesterday ©

Today's not gonna to be like yesterday

When I was upset with the world's own selfish way.

I was too blind to see

The selfish one was me.

And I met the girl with the sunshine eyes,

Who smiled so peacefully.

When she turned to speak, I realized that she couldn't speak clearly.

Well, she led me to a woman who couldn't talk quite right,

But she thinks as well as I can, so we sat and talked all night.

Today's not gonna be like yesterday,

When I was indifferent to the way people treat nature's harsh realities.

And one of those people was me.

For the children of today will be grown up tomorrow.

Who will show them the way, who will they follow?

But each one of them can weather life in some useful way,

If we all pull together to give them a chance today,

Today's not going to be like yesterday,

For I know there are many ways to help those less fortunate than we.

And won't you help them with me?

For inspiration to write this song, I went down to the Al Sigl Center in Rochester. The song is about the differently-abled people I met there, and it's also about me.

During the visit I became aware of how indifferent I had been to "disabled people", and wrote the line: "Today's not going to be like yesterday, when I was indifferent to the way people treat nature's harsh realities, and one of those people was me."

Little did I know that by a twist of fate, I would be one of "those" people a few years later. It is said that whenever you point a finger at someone else, three fingers point back at you. Did God bring back to me that which I was pointing to?

Whenever I think of, or listen to, that song, I feel that some part of me knew what my destiny was. Perhaps through that song, I was inviting into my life the opportunity to become differently-abled, therefore, God granted my request.

I am going to tell some of my life's story to try and give you a better perspective of the man I used to be, and how that contrasts with who I have become.

I graduated from Clarkson College in 1971 with a B.S. degree in Chemical Engineering. I was always near the top of my class. I went to work at Eastman Kodak Company, fell in love with a beautiful woman, and got married.

While I was working at Eastman Kodak Company as a chemical engineer, I also ran the Fantasy Mail Company from 1977-1979. It was one of the first mail order comic book companies in the country, and it was very successful. One year we achieved $100,000 in gross sales. That was a phenomenal amount for those times. Comics sold for about 25 cents, so you know we moved a lot of comic books that year. In 1980 I sold the Fantasy Mail Company and bought a restaurant and bar business with a partner; it was called "Mugs Up."

Trapped in a Fire...

January 4, 1981, started simply and ended tragically. Mugs Up was one of many businesses in a large downtown building. Being a Sunday and, therefore, closed to customers, I went to the basement office anticipating getting much done. Instead, my life was un-done.

Newspaper headlines the next day read, "Mugs Up owner hurt in fire." The fire started in the hallway to the office where I was and grew rapidly. There I lay, surrounded by flames, hidden in smoke, unconscious, trapped in the basement of a burning building. (The fire chief said the fire was "hotter than a pistol.") Firefighters had to extinguish the fire in order to get me out. It took them a while to find me because of the smoke and heat.

Carried out in a body bag...

At the time I weighed 250 pounds. The fireman had trouble carrying me; I don't know how he got me out. Miraculously, he did...in what looked like a body bag in the picture in the newspaper.

I first saw that newspaper picture many years later, while writing this book. As soon as I looked at it, I was overcome with emotion, because to me it looked like a dead man in a body bag being carried out on a stretcher. When I awoke from a coma after the fire, a doctor told me it was a medical miracle that I was alive. I was not burned, but the level of carbon monoxide in my body was enough to easily kill a person of my size.

The carbon monoxide poisoning caused a traumatic brain injury (TBI). This means that part of my brain functions; but my fine motor skills are gone. In addition to that, life-saving measures caused damage to my voice box, which have impaired my ability to speak clearly.

Motivated to Inspire Millions!

At first, I did not feel the miracle of being alive. Although I survived the fire, the life I knew was crumbling to its death. My already failing marriage ended in divorce. I was no longer able to function in my job at Eastman Kodak Company, and bankruptcy meant that I lost the Mugs Up business.

I felt hopeless, abandoned, and in despair at being labeled by society as "disabled." I felt my situation to be a curse. The resounding question in my heart was "Why did this happen to me?"

All that was familiar to me had changed, and I lived without purpose for years. These things hurt, but I was able to turn them around. Now, after over 30 years of re-evaluating this, of course, I can see that there is a great deal of good that came out of it. I see these things as the blessings they really are.

The reason this chapter is called "Disability: a Curse or a Gift from God?" is that I now believe that every thing and situation in our life is a gift. You have to learn to look at it from a different perspective, which I do. Everything can be considered a curse or a blessing. Sometimes in the moment it can feel like a curse, and it is only later, that it is felt as a blessing.

This was not easy for me to comprehend at first. My personal experience of struggling for years, enabled me to become passionate about helping others who may be stuck, so that they can shift into seeing their 'blessings' quicker than I did.

Ten years after the fire, I was awarded a settlement in a lawsuit against the city of Rochester. While I do get some assistance from the government, the award from winning this lawsuit is 60% to 70% of my monthly income. This is why I suggest to people, if they really do have just cause, to consider taking legal action for lost wages, because this can make a big difference in their lives.

When you don't feel forced to compete in the work place, you aren't concerned about where money comes from. Now I laugh about losing my job, because a job, a j-o-b, is 'just-over-broke', and anyone who understands that is laughing with me.

Having lost my job, this money allowed me to make changes in my life. For example, in where I was living. I also started collecting Jack Kirby artwork, which is part of my love for comic books. There were more possibilities, and also more challenges. The reason I see this as a blessing is that I now have the free time to do whatever I want to do.

What I felt at the time was the curse of losing my job, was turned around more than just 100% for me. If you just look at money, some people say that the job was a way to get money. However, if you get services from the government at no cost to you, this is a bonus way of having money. The money isn't given directly to you; many times, it's given as services.

Money is an exchange for a service given. When you go to the store to buy some prepared food, it's usually because you don't have time or want to make it yourself. When you buy a house, it's because you don't know how to build one yourself. You have to drive a car, because you don't know how to go out and create your own transportation.

This is an important point because people think they need money to survive. When you have a disability of some kind, what you actually need is service. You need a place to live, you may need someone to feed you, clothe you, help you bathe, and do any number of things. Everyone thinks you need money. You don't if you know how to avail yourself of the services the system provides for differently-abled people.

Winning the lawsuit was a big event in my life. However, an even more significant emotional and spiritual change happened even later, around 2001 or 2002, when I first saw the motivational speaker, Tony Robbins, on television.

Tony described how he went from an over weight nobody, to meeting and coaching people like President Ronald Regan I started listening to his tapes, and began believing that things would start changing for me; and they did.

The damage to my nervous system, which was caused from the carbon monoxide poisoning, affects my fine motor skills. Therefore, I have problems writing. I say that I can't write. You realize that when you say you can't do something, of course, you can't do it. People say "Frank don't say you can't do something, because then you can't do it." This is true, I can write, but it takes forever to write just a few sentences and to make it legible.

I began studying the Tony Robbins material extensively. I ordered a workbook from his organization and typed my answers in with my old Smith Corona typewriter. It was then that things started happening for me. I made a commitment to myself to attend several more Tony Robbins events.

During one event, I walked on burning hot coals. This comes from a guy who was trapped in a fire. You better believe I was scared to death to walk on fire, but I did it! I had the opportunity to repeat this at several other of his events and my feet were never burned.

That's when I found my purpose, and my destiny in life; and in so doing, I found myself. One of my missions in life is to serve others. It took me years to get to this point. It didn't happen overnight, even after meeting Tony Robbins. It happened over time.

Remember, when I first got TBI, one of the things that I felt was a curse was that I could no longer work as a chemical engineer for the Eastman Kodak Company. They hired me back for a little while, but my level of functioning was not what it needed to be for that position, so I had to return to being classified as "disabled". The blessing in this, is that by not having a conventional job, I can now invest all of my time and energy into doing things which will help others.

One of the blessings of having a TBI (traumatic brain injury) is that it got me in touch with my passion to help others, by giving love in any moment. If I did not go through my own ordeal of being differently-abled, I doubt that I would have this newly discovered passion.

Another blessing that I now have time for is to explore the passion I had for comic books when I was a little boy. Even though I ran a mail-order company that sold comic books, it was many years after my life changing experience, that my business partner and I started our own comic book company. I met my business partner at Tony Robbins events, and he made it possible for us to make the first issue of a comic book called "The Young Explorers"©.

The comic book is about the concepts I have learned from Tony Robbins, and all about my life. Every person has a hidden talent that may not come forth until they are put to the test. Of course, my comic books are written with children in mind. If kids can understand earlier in life what their hidden talents are, what they're passionate about, then they have a better chance at following their passion, and that's what my comic book is about. As a little boy, I was passionate about comic books. Now I am using comic books to help others follow their passion.

Because I believe so strongly in helping others, I also speak to audiences from people who are differently-abled, the unemployed, and even CEO's. My series of talks, which are the basis of the chapters in this book, were given at a place in Rochester, that helps people with 'disabilities', and is called PRALID.

A friend videotaped the talks for me. When I saw the recording of the first talk, I was appalled when I saw my hands moving uncontrollably because of my damaged fine motor skills. The next time I gave a talk, I held a full bottle in each hand, trying to control my hands by weighing them down. However, that just made things worse, because my hands still moved everywhere. The bottles were very distracting, so I put them down to finish the second talk. The point is that my passion to express something to help others was stronger than the feeling of being embarrassed. Because my passion, my reason for speaking, was very strong, I was able to express myself and just let go of everything else.

One thing I have noticed is that blessings always bring about more blessings. First there was the blessing of getting in touch with my passion for others. Then my passion for others became stronger than worrying about being embarrassed. This blessing, of being able to put my attention more on others than on myself, lead to the blessing of being able to do the series of talks.

Another thing I experience is short-term memory problems. This is great because, if someone does something bad to me, I can't remember it. Even long range I can't remember everything, which is also great. For example, I can't remember any of the painful personal stories that happened until I'm prompted to tell them, so I don't live in the past. This is one of the blessings of having a TBI. Everyone says, "Oh, I'm so sorry that this has happened to you." And I say, "I'm not, because everything turns out to be a positive!"

Related to this glitch in my memory, is the blessing that I focus on what I've got, instead of what I don't have. For example, I had a big comic book collection, which I sold to get a mortgage on the house I am now living in. Now that the comic book collection is gone, it doesn't clutter up my mind anymore. I still buy comic books, and I'm still attracted to Jack Kirby artwork, but the collection is gone. Instead, what I see and have gratitude for everyday is this home.

Something else that seemed like a curse was that I was not able to save my marriage. I was blessed because although I was losing my marriage, my ex-wife persisted in helping me adjust to having a TBI, by doing things such as inspiring me to complete all of the physical therapy, driving me places, and helping me pay my bills. Another blessing, that I discovered later, was that we aren't right for each other anymore. First of all, I have to be happy with who I am. This was a big shift for me. I am not dependent on someone else to make me happy. This freedom is a real blessing. I realized I must first be happy with myself, and then I will draw to me a woman who is happy on her own, and can complete the yin-yang process.

Losing time and focus for ten years had also seemed like a curse. I can't regain those hours, days, or years that I spent feeling sorry for myself. The blessing is that now I cherish every minute I have with someone. We all have a limited amount of time to live on this earth plane, so you have to manage time wisely. Spend your time on what is really important to you, and optimize your results. Otherwise, time will go away, it will disappear, and opportunities are lost.

Maximize whatever time and resources you have. The difference between a wealthy person and a poor person is that the wealthy person is maximizing his time and the use of his resources better, whereas a poor person is focused on something else, usually what they lack. "Wealth" is not only in money, but also in relationships, health, creativity, and spirituality.

Not being able to handwrite also felt like a curse to me. Writing by hand means that you are tapping into energy. Writing the words down yourself, is a way to connect with that energy. There are people who write their goals down on a card and carry it around in their pocket; they touch it, and they focus on what they have to do.

I experience a different kind of energy in the act of touching a keyboard than in holding a pen. There are times when I do not feel as connected. However, the blessing in not being able to write by hand, is that it has brought special people into my life to help me, whom I would not have met otherwise. For example, I couldn't write the manuscript for this book, which is why I had someone transcribing my recorded voice.

You can turn a lot of curses into blessings by bringing people into your life to assist you. Not being able to continue doing things you use to do, forces you to develop new skills. I have gotten really good at using a computer, and I reach out to many more people than I ever did before having a TBI.

Another thing I thought was a curse is that I am no longer able to sing well, because of the damage to my voice box. The blessing there is that it got damaged in the process of saving my life. The alternative would have been death. So, whenever I hear my voice, it is a reminder that I was given the blessing to live. I cannot be angry about that when I remember it saved my life. I've had over 30 years that I would not have had otherwise.

On Sundays, I sing in church. I sing as best I can, and I'm so joyful! This makes others joyful too. They look past my singing challenge, and respond to my happiness. This is a concept called "mirroring". Everything is a reflection to someone. For example, if you use the same posture and speech pattern as the person you are talking to, they will relate to you more easily and therefore, understand you better. If I'm talking to someone and they are getting what I'm saying, that means I'm reflecting energy to them at a level that is going to draw them to me, and they look past my voice challenge or my singing challenge.

Not being able to play the guitar, or to dance, because of my damaged nervous system, are other things that I felt were like curses. I can still strum a guitar, but I can no longer pick it. I can no longer play songs like Scarborough Fair/Canticle © by Simon & Garfunkel. If a woman leads, I can do a slow dance, but I can't do the dances I used to be able to, like the twist. I used to spend time doing both of these. The blessing is that now I am using my time on projects related to my passion to help others, such as writing this book.

I used to view my being judged as "disabled" as being a curse. The blessing is that, instead of focusing on being identified as "disabled", I turned it around by saying "differently-abled", and people are amazed, because in the greater scheme of things, it makes so much more sense. By being differently-abled, people come to help me, and I in turn help them, and that's a blessing!

If a crisis comes upon you, such as finding out that you have a brain injury or another illness, you have to find someone who can see the situation in a broader picture. Your family and friends and people who are close to you, may not understand what is happening. They may leave you. That just means that person didn't have the sensitivity or the patience to understand what you are going through.

Sooner or later, a person will come into your life who will understand and have a much better connection with you. For example, when I found the Center for Disability Rights (CDR), I found out that I can get services from them, and I am blessed to get this help. People come forth all the time that want to help me.

If you can see outside the box, you can see that everything does happen for a reason. It may not be what you want to have happen, but it has a purpose. You may have drawn something to yourself subconsciously. People say, "How can babies be born disabled? How can all of this happen?" I have no idea, but I feel that it is not a curse. If a child is born differently-abled, he doesn't know he is differently-abled, until he is exposed to the world. Therefore, he doesn't know what he does not have.

I know I have lost certain things by becoming differently-abled when I was 30 years old. However, I don't look back on that because of this memory problem. I don't think about what I lost, I choose to think about what I've gained.

If you are in a crisis right now, if you feel you have been cursed, or are in any way unfortunate, if that's why you're reading this book, please realize that you have more options. Do not get stuck focusing on what you have lost. You may have lost part of your brain function, your motor skills, or even your ability to feed yourself.

Seek someone out who can help you through this process. If you are able to step outside the crisis, there is a way to flip any problem around; there is always an alternative. There are people out there that want to help you. There are professional people in various agencies, who are trained to help you in your situation. Change your perspective 180 degrees, and things will get better. For me, that person was Tony Robbins, who inspired me over a number of years.

You have heard that time heals all wounds. It won't change you back and make you whole, to how you were before the injury, or whatever scenario has befallen you, but you can grow beyond the problem or grow into something better.

Do more than just 'get help' from someone, give something back to God and society. Get inspiration from Nick Vujicic (www.lifewithoutlimbs.org), who was born with no arms and no legs. See how happy he is, and how he changed his state of being. His message will touch you. He doesn't say, "God cursed me". He says that God blesses him, and that's how he inspires hundreds of thousands of people.

In Summary, there is a "gift" in every apparent "curse", which can be seen by stepping out of the crisis and taking on a new perspective. As you can see by my story, this process may take a long time, and you may need some help along the way. However, positive change is absolutely possible for you.

Action Steps for Chapter One

Disability: A Curse or a Gift from God?

- What are your limiting beliefs?
- In what ways do you feel differently-abled? Write this down.

- How is it a blessing? Write this down. You may need a friend to help you see it from a different perspective.

- Consider your passions, and how you might overcome the challenges that have blocked you from doing them. Write down your passions.

- What insight have you gained from reading this chapter? Write this down.

- List the things (job, people, activities) that used to consume you before becoming differently-abled, which you have "lost". How do you feel about each? Let go of your identity with how it looked before, and follow your passion from a new angle.

- Check out inspiring websites for a different perspective:
  www.lifewithoutlimbs.org /Nick Vujicic
  http://tinyurl.com/362m8o5/Liu Wei

Chapter Two

How I Turned my 'Disability' into an A$$et

An asset is defined as something that gives you cash flow. Your house isn't an asset unless you rent it. Your car isn't an asset unless you use it as a taxi to take people somewhere and they pay you money.

I turned my disability into an asset, by using services provided by the NY State Traumatic Brain Injury (TBI) Waiver Program. When thought of in terms of money, these services are an asset because someone else is paying money for them. I don't have to actually pay money for these services.

Service agencies project their revenues by their client base. As a client, you bring money to them from the Federal Government, which allows them to pay the staff and to have revenue. That means you are an asset to them! I see myself as being an asset to any agency who wants to provide me services.

Not everyone is as enthusiastic as I am about taking advantage of the opportunity to get these services. One of my biggest challenges with my friends who are in the TBI Waiver system is convincing them to fully use their 'TBI (Traumatic Brain Injury) Waiver staff.' They are there to serve you.

There are various staff roles. There is the HCSS (Home and Community Support Service), the ILST (Independent Living

Skills Trainer), the CIC (Community Integration Counselor) and the Service Coordinator. Each are paid anywhere from $11 to $40 an hour, but the Federal Government is charged approximately $20 to $70 an hour.

When you look at it that way, people in the TBI Waiver system receive tens of thousands of dollars in valuable services every year, in the form of people who want to help them. The degree to which you receive help is determined by the extent of your disabilities. Someone with extensive needs, such as 24-hour care, may even receive the equivalent of $100,000 a year, not in cash, but in services.

Everyone who has a stroke has suffered a Traumatic Brain Injury (TBI). Most of the people I know who have had a stroke don't want to apply for the TBI Waiver. They feel they don't need it, because they have retirement savings. I don't have that, but I did receive a settlement that was awarded to me. Even though I have this asset, I am still going to take advantage of the assistance the government offers. If God is going to provide me with the people and resources, then I will gratefully accept.

An important point is to see every person who comes to your house as if they are a blessing. They are there to help you.

The reason I say I have turned my disability into an asset, is because I am willing to accept the services that the TBI (Traumatic Brain Injury) Waiver program is willing to provide. Their service has a cash value, and this is an asset because they help me to grow, they help me to make exercise a priority, they help me eat properly, they drive me where I need to go, and they help me achieve new goals all the time.

I'm talking about using your 'staff' to leverage your time. For example, if you have to go out shopping, they can take you.

If you aren't capable of doing the shopping yourself, they have to do it for you. At the very least, they will assist you. It is even possible to have someone come and assist you with cleaning your house. Some people do not want this service; that means they aren't fully using the assets they are being offered. You will find that there are a variety of services that these agencies can provide, that you may have never considered. Once my staff even shoveled snow for me. They didn't shovel my driveway, but they had to shovel the walk so that they could get into my house. I live in Rochester, NY and we had 4 or 5 inches of snow. That's a safety hazard, so they shoveled the walk. The staff tries hard to keep things safe. I'm not saying you should abuse this privilege, but just think of not needing to do any of this stuff! It's going to free you up so that you can focus on accomplishing goals and growing in personal development.

This is why the subtitle to this book is about turning a disability into an asset. I want the reader to think of their 'staff' as being their asset. You are also an asset to these service agencies.

Action Steps for Chapter Two

How I Turned my "Disability" into an Asset.

- If you have a Traumatic Brain Injury (TBI), find out if there is a TBI Waiver Program in your state. It may be called something else. If there is, go through the application process. If necessary, set up a trustee so that you can have this help while keeping your financial resources.

- If you have another kind of disability, find out what federal/state/local programs you can apply for.

- Make full use of your 'staff' once you have them, and have an attitude of gratitude for their help.

- Could you be a speaker and help get the message out about how to prevent what happened to you? Speaking is a great way to help others, and you can get paid. This will take some research online, but can be worth it.

- Because of what you have gone through - do you see a tool, or invention you could design and patent that would help out someone in a similar condition as you. For example - the hook that grabs stuff from a cupboard for people in wheelchairs made someone a fortune.

- It is important to allow any of your emotions to arise. Then breathe through them and let them go.

Chapter Three

From Problems to Challenges to Opportunity

Just as every "curse" can be seen as a "gift", as illustrated in a previous chapter, every "problem" can be converted into a "challenge" and then to an "opportunity". This chapter focuses on thinking outside the box, so that you can look beyond your problems. There are always more choices than it may initially seem, and opportunities come when limiting beliefs are overcome. This can be an emotional process; it is important to allow emotions to arise and breathe through them without judgment. By being proactive, you can make significant changes in your daily life.

Everyone has problems. They come at inconvenient times, like when you have a flat tire. They come when your ATM card gets rejected. They come in various other ways too. However, every one of these can be converted from a problem into a challenge or opportunity. For example, if you are broke, you may not know where your money is going to come from. If you think there isn't enough money, then sure enough, this limiting belief is going to limit your accessibility to money. Actually, there is more than enough money for everyone.

For example, when my trustee helped me to buy this house, the mortgage wasn't initially approved because it is a unique property. The only way to get a mortgage on this house was for my trustee to come up with $150,000 in cash. I knew it could be raised, because my comic book collection was being sold at Heritage Auction through my trustee. My trustee was able to get a cash advance on the future earnings of the collection.

The real estate agent had thought this deal was dead in the water, because we weren't able to get a mortgage on it. I called her and said, "My trustee has a check for $150,000!" She asked how we got it, and I said, "We thought outside the box!"

If I looked at the failure to obtain a traditional mortgage as a problem only, I could have given up. I could have said, "Hey, I don't have the money to buy this house." Because I did not want to give up my dream, I turned this problem into a challenge. It was a challenge closing the deal to get the money, but it happened. I converted this into an opportunity. Now I have a tenant who pays rent; I have a beautiful house and I'm as happy as a pig in slop. I even have people come over that are amazed at what I have been able to do by changing a problem into a challenge, and then into an opportunity.

Before I had a trustee to manage my finances, a friend showed me a technique to use when I needed $10,000 cash to sign up for a Tony Robbins event. There are three courses: Date with Destiny, Life Mastery, and Wealth Mastery. They cost $5,000 each, or $10,000 for all three. I had no idea how I was going to get the money to do that. I didn't have $10,000 in my checking account.

This friend, who knew I wanted to go to these courses, called me up and said, "Frank, you bought a new car recently and paid cash for it. Go to the bank and take out a loan against it. You can pay the money back at an interest rate." I knew I could pay this back, so I did it, and I had the check. When I called to register for the courses and I said, "I have a check for $10,000. Do you want it?" the lady on the other end said, "Yes I do!"

Not everyone has a comic book collection to sell, or a new car to get a loan against. I am not advocating that everyone do this, or that anyone go into debt. However, you may have some other asset that could be converted into money. For example, it could be antiques or old coins that you could sell. I don't know what you have, but I'll bet you have something. If you're reading this and you have to find money, it is staring you in the face. It's not a pile of $100 bills; it has to be converted into that. But you have something of value to get out of this predicament.

For every problem, you have to think outside the box. When you stay inside the box, you are putting blinders on and not seeing your opportunities. You'll have to either get a friend to help coach you through the process, or get outside your body. You have to go into your spirit, and your heart (feeling), you have to say "God" (universe, or whatever you are comfortable with), "There has to be something I am not seeing here."

This is where your 'Scooby Ears and Eyes' come in, which I talk about in a later chapter.

You have to suspend your limiting belief that there is no solution to whatever the current problem is. Once you do, it will become obvious what you should do. It could be a drug addiction, financial issues, a marital or relationship problem, etc. Every problem can be converted into a challenge or an opportunity, but only if you think outside the box.

Let's use the example of an unhealthy relationship. Perhaps your spouse has been assaulting you. If you're married, you may think you have no place to go. People are usually afraid of change, and don't want to admit that they need help to get out of their situation. They don't realize it, but there are people who are trained to help them get out of being in an abusive relationship. Or if you have a drug addiction, there are people who can help you, but you have to be willing to 'get outside the box'.

Only then can you see the various opportunities that you have around you. For instance, if you are addicted to smoking, there are many options that can help you. You have to get focused. If you say, "I can't do this," then of course you can't. Change your mindset, or you will miss an opportunity to move outside the box.

Once you realize that you have other choices, you move from having a problem to having a challenge. Once you start overcoming this problem, opportunities will come, and you can teach someone else how to do this. For example, you could become a motivational speaker; you never know. If you're in debt and you find a way out of it, you could become a debt counselor. You create these opportunities by converting a problem into a challenge.

The opportunities will come to you. It doesn't matter what obstacles or challenges you have – the opportunities will come, and usually in unexpected ways. For example, when I bought this house I never thought I would be helping a tenant. I find that she can help me too. There is a reason for everything.

Recently, I spoke with someone who was focusing on some problems. I suggested that she breathe deeply in and out repeatedly, until she was no longer focused on the problem. Facing a problem can be very emotional. When a person gets emotional, it is usually because they are revisiting a time when something bad or something good happened in their lives, and they are recalling the emotions that were present at the time. You can't predict what a person is going to say. It can come out as love or anger or something else.

One time, while I was giving the talk "Turning a Problem into a Challenge and then into an Opportunity," a woman got very emotional and began swearing. She had a Traumatic Brain Injury (TBI), and has a harder time speaking than I do. She was so frustrated at her inability to speak, that she started to swear. An event worker came over and started admonishing her for doing it, attempting to quiet her. I said to the aide, "It's okay, she's okay; she just got emotional revisiting her past."

"Its okay to be emotional; thank God we can cry. Share what you are feeling; let it go. You are very courageous. I'm not upset you swore, sometimes I swear too."

With every problem, you have to go back to the root of why it occurred. You have to feel it, and experience it on a deeper level in order to understand why this happened to you. Sometimes, you may be so overwhelmed by the emotional loss, you may swear, but it is all part of the process.

Some people with a TBI, who are in the TBI Waiver system, say that their staff is not as helpful as they could be. However, it is usually a client's lack of self worth that keeps them from speaking up about this. For example, if your aide does not show up, be more proactive, and call the agency and ask what happened, and see if they are able to send out a replacement. If not, then I suggest that you make better use of the unexpected time by either reading a book or calling up a friend, not whine and complain, but just be present in the moment.

I used to be content with whomever they would send me, because I just needed some company. Eventually, I became more assertive, and demanded that they not send me aides who were just there to babysit me. It is sometimes a challenge for agencies to find dedicated people as staff, who really care about their clients. At least, that was my experience. Once I understood the system better by being more proactive, I began getting better service.

In summary, every "problem" can be converted into a "challenge" and then to an "opportunity", just by taking on a different perspective. This can be emotional, so breathe through any difficulty, as long as it takes. Remember to be proactive, and ask someone to give an objective opinion as to what other choices you have. Be open to letting go of limiting beliefs, and be alert to notice the opportunities that will certainly come.

Action Steps for Chapter Three

From Problems to Challenges to Opportunity

- Make two columns on a piece of paper. On the left, write down "problems". On the right, write down "opportunities" for each problem. Fill in the columns. Ask someone to help, if you get stuck.

- What do you have that can be turned into money, or traded for services?

- Save your answers to these Action Steps, so that you can refer to them during the chapter on Goal Setting and Achieving.

- Check out this book: 'Don't Sweat the Small Stuff', by Richard Carlson.

Chapter Four

Scooby Ears and Eyes

Previous chapters spoke of the positive results that can occur when you are able to take on a different point of view. This chapter focuses on a particular technique, that will greatly help you develop this skill. It is called using your "Scooby Ears and Eyes", which I learned about at a Tony Robbins event. This term comes from the cartoon, "Scooby Doo, Where Are You?" Scooby Doo had ears that shot up whenever he sensed danger, or something like that. This technique develops your naturally occurring Reticular Activating System (RAS) to filter out what is important to you. In this way, you get what you focus on.

As your sensitivity grows, you will become more aware of themes in your life that are repeated patterns. You will learn to realize when you are drawing something positive or negative to yourself, which values you are moving toward, and which values you are moving away from. The more you understand and notice how your RAS works, the more quickly you will be able to see the blessings and opportunities in your life. At the end of this chapter are Action Steps, to get you started on developing your own Scooby Ears and Eyes.

Scooby Ears and Eyes activate your "Reticular Activating System" (RAS), which is part of your brain. Every minute you have a million different impulses that go to your brain. They come primarily from your sight, but they also come from your other senses, smell, taste, touch, and hearing.

Your brain cannot filter everything out at once. So your RAS, or your Scooby Ears, filter the things that are most important to you; what you focus on in any given moment.

Remember that you get what you focus on. For example, if you buy a new car, you start to see it everywhere, because it's important to you. Until then, you saw a million cars on the street. You don't recognize the one that's yours until you own it. It's the same with a woman who buys a purse or a new dress. She thinks it's unique until she sees a friend or a neighbor with the same purse or dress. That's because it's important to her, and so that is why you get whatever you focus on.

Why does this matter to you? You will get better results by listening, watching, and learning from those around you, to develop and use these new skill sets. You may need someone who can help you to improve your life in some way. Everybody gives off different energy vibrations. Everybody transmits energy at a certain frequency and your Scooby Ears, your reticular activating system, actually senses this.

Your Scooby Ears and Eyes and Antennas are working all the time. This can work for anything. For example, this is how I found an ILST (Independent Living Skills Trainer) at the YMCA. One day while there, I saw a thin woman exercising.

"I'll bet you're an ILST, aren't you," I inquired.

"Yes, how did you know?"

"It's the way you carry yourself; it's something about your energy. God puts people in my life for a reason," I responded.

I was using my Scooby Ears and Eyes, filtering the energy that she was emitting. She was an ILST, and she came to work for me. You can use your 'Scooby Ears and Eyes' for the TBI Waiver system too. If you're in the system and you have staff members, use your Scooby Ears and Eyes to get top quality ones.

You need to be alert and aware, and you have to know your goals. Then, take action, follow up, and enjoy the journey. Notice if something shows up in your life over and over again. The universe, or God, or whatever your term for it, is trying to get your attention.

For example, the pastor at church talked about the movie, "Fireproof." Then a year later, "Fireproof" was mentioned again. It was brought to my attention twice. So I got this movie, watched it, and it changed my life. I said "God, I'm willing to do whatever you are trying to have me do, by looking to you today." He got my attention!

Focus on what you are interested in. When I do, other things fall away. I'm interested in Jack Kirby because he created comic books. When I look at a comic book, if it has his image on it, or I recognize his artwork, I'm more likely to be attracted to it. There hasn't been a new comic book of his published since he passed away ten years ago. This means I usually have to search for old comic books that he produced. I have learned to do that by separating his images from other artists he worked with at the time, such as Paul Reinman, Don Heck, etc.

To review a few points, your Scooby Ears are your reticular activating system. When I say, "you get what you focus on," this can apply to anything. If you want to become good at doing anything, focus on it. You have to use your Scooby Ears and Eyes and your reticular activating system. Next, eliminate all distraction to becoming whatever it is that you want to do. For example, if you want to become a good father, then read and study books on fatherhood. If you know of a father you admire, use him as a role model. If your goal is to be the best loving husband you can be, you should study what it takes to become one.

As another example, suppose you want to buy a car, but the price is outside of your comfort zone, such as a Rolls Royce. That means you have to focus on it; visualize it in your mind. Pick out a model that you are drawn to without looking at the price. Notice the energy it gives off. You will find that same energy coming from similar styled vehicles with a much better price tag.

That's why I bought a 2013 Hyundai. I had previously owned several Hyundai Sonatas because they had features that reminded me of a Jaguar. I have owned Sonatas built in 2005, 2008, 2010, and 2013. This means you are very likely to get what you focus on.

For example, my assistant, Marvelous Michele, saw me drinking a diet green tea. She picked it up and said, "Frank, there's Aspartame in this; this isn't good for you." While she did this, there were also flowers sitting on the table, a book, her computer, paperwork, an unfinished puzzle, and other things. Although she saw all of this, her mind filtered out everything except that bottle. She picked it up, realized there was an additive in it that wasn't healthy for me, and said something about it. Why? It is because she is focused on living a healthy lifestyle, and my health is important to her. She wants to make a difference in my life by using her Scooby Ears and Eyes.

For those who have a TBI, and are getting help through the TBI Waiver system, remember to use your Scooby Ears and Antennas to get the best help available. I choose everyone who works for me by using my Scooby Ears and Eyes, and so can you. Some people can offer more of their time, more enthusiasm, and more of their love, than others. Unfortunately, there are always some who are just there to do a job.

Using your Scooby Ears and Eyes is easy if it's about something that you're interested in. This means that in relationships, you drew to yourself your partner using the same system. You may think that you had no say in it, but you did manifest this person in your life.

If you aren't careful, you could manifest the wrong person, so be aware of your values. There is another technique I learned about through Tony Robbins, which he calls "moving towards values" and "moving away values". You can rank these values and use your Scooby Ears and Eyes to attract that partner. There may be twenty qualities you want a woman to have. For example, the 'moving towards values' could be that she is beautiful, a great cook, loves kids, is your best supporter, and is at peace with her inner self. In other words, positive uplifting values. The 'moving away values' could be that she drinks or smokes, and so on.

Ranking these values gives you clarity on what you want to have in your life. Would you rather have a beautiful wife who did possibly smoke? What would be more important to you? When you have clarity, your Scooby Ears will filter it out. Most people don't do this when they meet a potential mate, they just go along with whatever emotion they're feeling in the moment. This can cause them serious challenges later on in their life.

This is how Scooby Ears and Eyes work. They filter the things that you want from those that you don't. For example, in the beginning of a relationship, a woman may put aside or ignore the fact that a man doesn't pick up around the house. That could be overlooked in the shadow of being 'in love', until she gets tired of picking up after him every day. That means that her reticular activating system, when they first got into the relationship, was focused on the positive, fun things, and she later became focused on the negative aspects.

From the opposite perspective, if you focus on the negative, that's what you're going to get more of – negative issues. If you focus on the positive, you will get positive things back. You can reframe the entire relationship, depending on what you focus on.

To summarize the key points of this chapter, your Scooby Ears and Eyes use your RAS (Reticular Activating System) to draw to you the things you focus on. This is already happening, and the more you become aware of it, the more you will be able to develop the skill of intentionally focusing on getting your desired outcome.

Action Steps for Chapter Four

Scooby Ears and Eyes

- Notice when you use your Scooby Ears and Eyes. When was the last time you did this? Write this down.

- Make a list of your "moving towards" values, which are things that attract you.

- Make a list of your "moving away" values, which are things that repel you.

- Write down something that you want in your life that seems out of your reach, and keep focusing on it, until you find something similar (like what I did in buying a car that reminded me of a Jaguar because an actual Jaguar was out of my budget for now).

Chapter Five

Using Adversities to Discover Hidden Talents

Yes, you have a hidden talent, waiting to be uncovered! I have noticed that when people start converting problems into opportunities, and using their Scooby Ears and Eyes, they face tests. These tests bring out hidden talents that were not seen before, because people become creative and use their natural passion to overcome adversities.

Some talents were previously disguised as liabilities. Often, the talent is related to a passion, which had been suppressed. Following a passion can propel you through any difficulty, because it gives you a desire strong enough to make the change happen. As you make changes to develop your talent, you may hit a wall, or many walls. This is part of the test, and the catalyst that is part of developing the talent. Regardless of your age, always go back to your passion for the strength to proceed.

Everyone was given multiple talents that they may not fully realize until they are tested. A test may mean that a life-changing event has happened. For me, the event was becoming differently-abled, and through this test I discovered the hidden talent of being a motivational speaker with a passion to help others.

Out of every adversity comes a turning point, that some may call a test. If you have a broken marriage, if your husband or wife leaves you, maybe you got pulled over for drunk driving, or it could be as simple as not being happy in your current situation; whatever it is, could be the turning point, the pivotal point in your life, when you make the decision to move forward in your life in a positive way.

Everything happens for a reason. This means that every obstacle you run into is an opportunity. A test is when you bump up against a wall in your life. It is the opportunity for you to ask yourself, "What should I be learning from this?" Instead of focusing on the wall you are facing, focus on how to creatively change the situation.

A hidden talent that I discovered for myself is the ability to connect with people at a deeper level than what goes on in most people's conversations. It's like peeling the layers of an onion back to the core. The challenge is finding ways to creatively reach people in order to help them.

However, once a hidden talent is discovered, it must be developed. Use your Scooby Ears and Eyes to find ways to do this. There will be adversity, but other possibilities will open.

In my particular case, I had someone write a movie script that I hoped to promote at a Tony Robbins event. It didn't work out at that time, but I got a call much later from the man who was to become my business partner. He had noticed me at the event, and contacted me, saying, "I want to make this dream of yours come true, of making this movie." He told me about relatively small companies that made comic books into movies.

Up to that point, I had collected and sold comic books, but I had not created one myself. With my business partner's help, we published the first issue of a comic book, called "The Young Explorers ©". My partner showed me how to get past the adversities of not being able to handwrite, or draw, by using other resources to get these parts done. The right person will always come into your life at the right time, and things will begin to happen.

The storyline of "The Young Explorers ©" is this: There are five kids, who get assigned to join a Commodore on a dangerous mission to complete certain tasks. During the group's mission, they go though many tests. With each test, a hidden talent of one of the kids is revealed. You don't know what's going to happen until they are confronted with each task.

For example, one kid speaks in a pigmy language. No one else can understand him, and at first this seems like a problem. However, he ends up saving the entire crew when they go to an island that speaks only Pigmy, and he is the only one who speaks the language fluently.

Sometimes our talents are disguised as liabilities, and this may not be obvious until we are put to a test. If you're tested when you are a little kid, you can often find what you are passionate about, what you want to do for the rest of your life. This becomes a 'turning point'.

However, if you aren't careful, your kid dreams could remain just kid dreams, and not grow into passions. Every kid's passion should be followed, except for destructive tendencies. Although all tendencies, even negative traits, can be turned into a positive passion.

Most people either forget their passions or ignore them. If someone has a job that they don't like doing, I would say, "What did you like to do when you were a little boy or a little girl?" Let's say that when they were little, pets were very important to them, but they aren't pursuing their desire to enjoy pets. They are doing something that is completely out of line with who or what they wanted to be when they were growing up, until a shift occurs, such as losing their job.

Their passion for pets could turn into a career goal. They could become a veterinarian, and perhaps own a hospital for dogs, cats, parrots, or snakes, etc. They could work at a wildlife preserve or become an animal activist; maybe even become the zoo master. Any of these might fulfill their childhood dreams.

Following your passion can propel you through any difficulty. By the time you're 40, you undoubtedly have a spouse, children, a mortgage, car payments, or other obligations. You have had to make it a real priority to figure out how to meet those needs. What if your needs were met by doing what you are passionate about? Our passions are what we are meant to do; they can also generate income for you. It's not just about making money; if you follow what you are passionate about, the money will come to you, believe me.

It's never too late; it just becomes more of a challenge when you are older. Let's say a man has been making $50,000 to $100,000 a year and then goes to zero; boom, he has lost his job. He knows that whatever he was doing to make money isn't working for him anymore. This means he has to be resourceful enough to think outside the box, as he still has obligations to meet. Being resourceful means he needs to network, to maintain a close relationship with his wife, with his spirit, with his God, and to see that things happen for a reason.

Now, I've been saying, "have to or needs to", but it is really a "want to". "Have to", sounds like you are being forced in some way, and that isn't going to work. It is the feeling, the passion, the wanting to, that is going to make the change possible.

Let's say you do have someone in your life, such as a spouse and/or children. This could be a double-edged sword. It could propel you to move forward, or it could make you give up entirely. It will depend on how you perceive it. Every adversity comes for a reason; and you should know that it's a test for you to see what you're made of, and discover your hidden talents. Maybe you weren't meant to be a stockbroker, or a real estate agent, or a construction worker. Perhaps you were meant to help people, perhaps you were meant to be an animal lover, or an actress, or something else. Maybe you wanted to be in movies when you were a kid, or become a ballet dancer. Perhaps you couldn't follow that path, because you didn't have the money to pursue it. Had you followed your passion from when you were a little kid, your life would have taken an entirely different path from what it is now.

Whenever you are faced with adversity, you bump up against a wall; you need to take two or three steps back and breathe. Some of us have a tendency to think we have to figure out why this adversity happened, and where in the past our journey went wrong. In reality, it does not matter how you got to this point. What matters is what actions we are going to take to change the current situation. It means we consciously modify our behavior from here on out.

It doesn't mean that you will necessarily over react by taking drastic measures, but it does mean that you follow what spirit advises you to do. Listen to what the universe is trying to tell you. For example, I would not want a person to think, "Hey, if I get pregnant, I'll just get an abortion." That might be your choice, but is it the right choice for you? Don't let it be your first choice, make an informed decision. Find out what this is going to mean for you for the long term.

Every adversity reveals a hidden talent. For example, if you were a party to an unwanted pregnancy, somehow, there was a reason it worked out the way it did. God or the universe is giving you the gift of discernment to understand the choices you make. The hidden reason will reveal itself, once you discover why you made that choice. You will then use that to change the situation and allow it to become one of growth.

This is an allegory for life. You've probably already run into a great challenge in your life, and you say, "Hey, I didn't realize I was being tested." You could be differently-abled and you don't realize why you became differently-abled. You could be in a marriage in which you are unhappy; you could be broke. Wherever you are at in your life, there will be a turning point that will show you what you are made of.

In summary, you have a hidden talent, or perhaps many hidden talents, which will become discovered as you overcome adversities. Tapping into a passion, perhaps a passion from childhood, can give you the strength it will take to pursue developing newly discovered talents.

Action Steps for Chapter Five

Using Adversities to Discover Hidden Talents

- What did you like to do when you were little? What captivated you? Write this down.

- What are you doing now to follow your passions? Write this down.

- Make two columns on a sheet of paper. On the left put adversities. On the right put the hidden talents you have learned or have the potential to learn from each adversity.

- Check out the Passion Test: www.thepassiontest.com

Chapter Six

Fantastic is My Brand

"Branding" is a powerful tool that you can use to reinforce the changes you make as you recognize blessings, see opportunities, and develop hidden talents. My first experience with and exposure to branding, was through comic books. Later I saw that branding is used globally in marketing, so that a product will be recognized and remembered.

You can create a brand for yourself in order to reinforce positive changes you have made, and to help others support these changes, because our minds and bodies are affected by words. When I introduce myself by saying, "I am Fantastic Frank", my state of 'being' changes to one of ecstasy and joy, and the person I am speaking with is also affected.

The creators of the comic books I collected when I was a little boy had brands. However, they weren't called brands then; they were called monikers or 'handles'. Stan Lee, of Marvel Comic Books, branded himself "Stan The Man Lee", and he also branded "Jack The King Kirby". Stan Lee branded everybody, including his secretary. Everybody who worked at Marvel Comic had a brand name. In 1961 Stan The Man Lee created, with Jack The King Kirby, the Fantastic Four, Spider Man, X-Men, the Avengers and the Incredible Hulk, just to name a few of them.

Many years later, I meet Frank Gasiorowski, and was on regular conference calls with him and a group of others whom he was mentoring. On one of his morning calls, Frank suggested reading a book called *"Differentiate or Die"*. In this book, they talk about Coca Cola, "Coke - The Real Thing"; that's a brand. The little symbol that looks like a bolt of lightning is the brand of Nike shoes. Everything needs to be branded out in the world in order to be recognized and remembered. This is why I was inspired to brand myself.

The first time I used "Fantastic Frank" was on one of those morning calls with Frank Gasiorowski. It was not my intent to introduce myself that way; it was spontaneous. I said, "Hi, I'm Fantastic Frank", and it has stuck ever since. That's how I got branded. My comic book says it was created by "Fantastic Frank".

Since I had previously studied the power of words through my contact with Tony Robbins, I knew that how I responded to a question, such as, "How are you?" would indeed become my experience. It causes my body to snap into a state of pure joy and ecstasy. Embracing my brand has allowed me to be who I really am, instead of letting my disability define who others tell me I am. If I live my life as "Disabled Frank", that means I am disabled. When I live as "Fantastic Frank", that is exactly who I become.

The body and mind can be heavily affected by the words you use. For example, I never use the words "depression", "down", or "unhappy" to describe myself. That is because the words you use will actually change your physical state and mind. Taking control of language can actually change how you feel about yourself, your situation, and everything else. This is why, whenever I am asked how I am doing, no matter what I am feeling, my response is always, "I am FANTASTIC"!

Even though I am "differently-abled", I often wear a T-shirt, that I had made, which says, "I am empowered by GOD".

Why? Because "disabled" has negative 'anchors' attached to it. A better way to describe me is to say "differently-abled", which I like much better as a label, than being "disabled." So, to say I am "empowered by God" is a type of branding.

When considering a brand for yourself, pay attention to how it sounds. Compare it to other titles of brands that you like the sound of. I personally, liked the sound of the "Fantastic Four", which was a comic book I read for over 20 years. I modeled the sound of my brand, "Fantastic Frank" from the "Fantastic Four". They are alliterations, in that the words begin with the same sound. It sounds better than "Amazing Frank" or "Fabulous Frank". "Fabulous Frank" sounds a bit too female to me. "Fantastic Frank" just has the right flow to it - "FAAAN-TAS-TIC FRANK".

My father's name was Francis. "Fantastic Francis" doesn't sound great, because "Francis" has too many syllables, but "Fantastic Frank", with Frank being one syllable, fits very well. This was a process for me. I like to give monikers, or brands, to people I meet. I've given my lovely assistant, Michele, the name "Marvelous Michele." When I meet a woman named Angela, I might say, "How about being Amazing Angela"? It is a play on words and it depends on the flow. Another way of looking at it is that Fantastic Frank just sounds better than anything else, like Helpful Frank, or Amazing Frank, or Beautiful Frank. Beautiful Beth might be something that works for a Beth. 'Fantastic Frank' just works for me. I am so blessed to be named Frank.

It is important to be sensitive to each situation; make sure it is appropriate to use your brand, and how much emphasis to put on it. For example, I had a little trouble stating with enthusiasm, "I'm FANTASTIC", when I was at my Uncle Bob's funeral. People came up to me, and asked me how I was doing. I wanted to say "FANTASTIC!" but I had to say "fantastic" in a lower voice, out of respect for my Uncle Bob. There are certain times when we need to be more discrete.

You can use branding in your own life by developing your own personal brand. This will help you as well as others, focus on your passion and the positive changes you are making. My brand is "Fantastic Frank" – what is yours?

Action Steps for Chapter Six

Fantastic is My Brand

- Pick a brand for yourself, and have fun with it. For example, I made my license plate "FANTASTK".

- Read this book: *Differentiate or Die: Survival in Our Era of Killer Competition*, by Jack Trout

- Start using your brand when introducing yourself, on your email signature, on your business card, etc.

Chapter Seven

Move from Depression to an Improved State of Mind

One theme throughout this book has been the power of words. This chapter focuses on this topic, and extends it to include your environment, people, and anything else that is important to you. However, use caution, because a word habitually used to describe oneself, even if done unconsciously, such as saying that you are "depressed", becomes a part of your identity.

Your state of mind can be improved dramatically by using words that shift you from a negative state to a positive one. It is also important to surround yourself with positive people, a positive environment, and to minimize time focusing on negative subjects. Taking action and helping others is another way to shift to a 'happier' state.

Depression; what is depression? There are various definitions. Many definitions include words such as sadness, gloom, dejection, dullness, withdrawal, pessimistic sense of inadequacy, and sometimes, even suicidal tendencies.

That may seem to be a 'depressing' list of definitions. My favorite definition is "a low state of vital powers". This means that you have a low emotional and energetic state, which does not have quite the negative connotation as dejection, gloom, and being suicidal. In other words, your energy's vibrational level is low.

The words that you use have 'anchors', which can be internal or external in nature. The term 'anchor' implies that something has a deeper meaning to a person than just the definition of the word. It triggers a particular emotional state, positive or negative.

'Habitual' means repeated. We are often unaware of how frequently we use certain words, out of habit, and the impact this has. If you use words habitually to describe yourself, you will become branded with them, and they will become your identity. That's why I choose to be called "Fantastic Frank" as my brand. That's why one of my T-shirt reads, "I am empowered by God," not, "I am disabled by God".

This is also another reason why you should avoid words like "depressed" or "disabled" to describe yourself. These terms, while they may mean different things to different people, do not empower you or I when we use them. A better choice of words to describe one's self, would be 'blessed,' or 'differently-abled'.

Now, why would a 'disabled' person want to call themselves 'differently-abled'? If someone comes up to you and asks if you are disabled, you can say, "I am differently-abled". That causes a brain schism in the other person, and they can't understand 'differently-abled'. They try and figure out what this means, and then they try to decide if you are "abled" or "disabled."

Most people would not understand the phrase TBI or Traumatic Brain Injury. Therefore, there is no need to use it to describe yourself, when you will then have to go into an explanation of what it means, which may be more unnerving to you than it's worth. Instead of saying you have a TBI, say you are 'differently-abled'.

If you are asked what 'differently-abled' means, you can tell them about the blessings and hidden talents that you have discovered. This will shift the focus of the conversation away from your challenges and onto more positive topics.

"How you can improve your happiness?" This relates to shifting from a negative state to a positive one.

For example, I found an old notebook I had forgotten about from before I had my TBI. In it, I had written many love songs about the anguish of losing love. Re-reading those old songs, made me realize that I don't want to be in that state anymore.

One way to get rid of a negative emotional state is by writing down the emotions you are experiencing. The act of writing them out, frees your mind to focus on other things. I lost the use of my fine motor skills, so I use a computer to type instead of writing them by hand. Next, I suggest you tear up what you have written down about these depressing emotions, or burn them. In this way, you are less likely to go back to them, and your old program of reliving them is gone.

So, writing things down and letting them go is one way to improve your happiness. There are other things you can do, too. Listening to music, reading an inspiring book, and positive social interaction, are all great ways to change your state of mind.

Focusing on helping another person will take your attention off of yourself. Your brain can't occupy two thoughts at the same time. If you are really listening to someone else, you won't be thinking about your own problems or be depressed. When you talk to someone, make eye contact with them, because the eyes are the windows to the soul. Every time you make eye contact, you can connect with them through their energy field. If a person is happy or sad, you can see it in their eyes.

A good staff person (of service) will notice that you are down or depressed, anxious, or that something else is going on. You convey it through your body language, the way you talk, the way you look, your facial expression, and your eye contact. Your aide should be able to assist you in pulling yourself out of a negative state of mind.

If you have a TBI and are receiving services, please maximize the use of every person who works with you, whether it's an ILST (Independent Living Skills Trainer), HCSS (Home and Community Support Service), a CIC (Community Integration Counselor), a supervisor, or someone else in the system. It is especially good to use them in a time of crisis.

The people that you surround yourself with in your daily life should be positive and help you to raise your morale. You don't want to be around people who are negative, condescending, or who tell you that you can't do things. You want to be around people who are going to uplift you, not limit you. This could be a challenge if you are in a difficult marriage, or living with an unsupportive family, but there are certain things you can do. Reflecting as much happiness as you can will let that light shine through. Seek out a counselor or clergyperson you trust. They can help you, but you have to first be aware of the fact that you need help. Some people may become so deeply depressed, that they don't even realize that they need help to raise their energy vibration.

Your environment means everything. "Environment" includes things you watch, listen to, read, and surround yourself with. Most of the stories on the news or radio are about rapes, murders, robberies, disasters, and people having trouble; all negative energy. Bob Proctor told a story of a newspaper out in LA that went under. It printed just good news, and it went under because no one paid to advertise in it. Sadly, many people would rather focus on bad news than good news.

Of course, you want to be informed as to what is going on worldwide. Find a way to get just enough information to keep yourself aware, but do not become obsessed with watching the news, reading the newspaper, or listening to the radio. If you feel you are becoming overly concerned with what is happening in the world, shift your focus onto something uplifting.

In summary, this chapter reinforced the power of words on your emotional state, and the importance of not using words such as 'depressed' to describe yourself. Improving your state of mind can start with a shift in your words, and can extend to your environment, the people you surround yourself with, the amount of negative information you take in, and the degree to which you use your energy to help others.

Take notice of what you are focusing on. If you focus on the negative, this is what your life will become. If you focus on being and doing happy things, then your life will become one of happiness. Surround yourself with the best people who can help you, and above all else, remain focused on your passion.

Action Steps for Chapter Seven

Move from Depression to an Improved State of Mind

- Notice words that put you in a bad mood. Write them down. Replace them with empowering words. Right these down, and start using them daily.

- Ask a friend, family member, or aide, to tell you what negative words they notice you using a lot, and to help you track how often you use the new empowering words instead.

Chapter Eight

Goal Setting and Goal Achieving

As you get in touch with your passion, something specific that you want to achieve will begin to take shape. When this occurs, it is time to set a goal. Different approaches to goal setting and goal achieving are covered in this chapter; take the one that works best for you and go with it.

There is a lot of useful information within this chapter, so take the time to study it thoroughly for maximum benefit. I suggest that you first read the chapter through to get a feeling of the full content, and then go back to specific points that you want to concentrate on. At any point in the process, having someone such as a mentor to guide you will be a great help. Mentoring is discussed more fully in a later chapter.

Why set goals? Well, there are many different reasons to set goals.

One that I like is: To achieve or to maximize the sense of wellness in any area of our lives, we have to set goals.

Another is more metaphysical (meaning, 'beyond the physical') in nature: Since we are all not yet perfect creations in our own perspective, it is our inherent nature to need to improve on ourselves.

Then there is the non-metaphysical side: We always want more of something. It may be more money, it may be more time, it may be more love, or it may be more health. There is usually something that we want to change or feel we lack.

We all face obstacles, or barriers, as we travel our individual paths on our journey back home. Even in a race, you have a starting point and a finishing point. Without a plan or a map, you may not reach your destination. Having a goal and making a plan, helps us move towards what we desire.

Many people will set a new goal every New Year, but fail to make a plan to reach it. After a few months into the New Year, most have given up on it or don't even remember what the goal was. There are two aspects to making a goal manifest. One is goal 'Setting', and the other is "Achieving"; both are required. 'Goal Setting' is an intellectual process, while 'Goal Achieving' is emotional. Goal setting involves having a plan, which I will cover using the SMART goals model. Goal achieving very often happens spontaneously, without a specific plan. For example, you may have the goal of getting a great used car. You may spontaneously see the perfect car for you as you drive down the street, with a "For Sale" sign. You didn't even need to search advertisements or visit new car dealers.

All that is required is that you give it up to the universe, knowing that when the time is right, you must take inspired action to achieve your goal.

You may need someone to help you follow the steps described in this chapter, to develop your own personal goal plan. My coach, Frank Gasiorowski, or 'Mr. 90 Day Goals', helps me with his program. Here is an outline of the simple steps that will help you avoid getting mixed or weak results. This process uses the model of 'SMART GOALS'. Each step will be described in more detail after this outline.

Step 1: Make a list of goals, and pick one to work on.

Step 2: Answer the question: Who? (Whose goal is it?)

Steps 3 - 7: Go through the SMART of "SMART GOALS":

S = Specific (What? Why? How?)

M = Measurable

A = Achievable

R = Realistic

T = Timely

Step 8: Consider the GOALS of "SMART GOALS":

G = Greatness

O = Open minded

A = Attitude

L = Learning

S = Success

Step 9: Have a mentor review your goal plan, and be accountable to them.

Now, for the directions:

Step 1: Make a list of goals, and pick just one to work on.

It is important to have a written goal, because it will help you to focus on and achieve it. This step should be fun. Brainstorm and write down things you have longed for in your life. They can be related to any area of life: personal growth, family, health, money, business, spirituality, etc.

Having too many goals at once can be overwhelming, and a challenge to stay focused on, because you cannot work on every goal at the same time. I started out with ten or more goals, which my ILST (Independent Living Skills Trainer) shortened into a more manageable number of about five. Then my private therapist got it down to three basic ones, which I am constantly improving. They are: Exercising, Eating, and Sleeping. Each goal has related sub-goals under them. For instance, my three basic goals all relate to how I best utilize my time. Pick the goal that best describes something you are passionate about and write it down.

Step 2: For the chosen goal, answer the question: Who?

Sometimes we allow others to set goals for us. For example, our parents set goals for us when we were little, such as to walk, to talk, to become potty trained, etc. When we went to school, we all had goals which we were to achieve. Every teacher had to have a goal plan for us, even if we were not aware of it. You may recall all of those parent-teacher conferences, and your report cards.

Whose goal is it? Is it yours? Or did someone else make it for you? Is it worth investing yourself in order to get the perceived benefits from it?

It can't be your aide's, your father's, your brother's, your sister's, or your mother's; it has to be your goal because unless it's your goal you may never do it. If the goal you chose is not yours, go back to Step 1 and choose a different goal.

Step 3: S = Specific (What? Why?)

Now that you have chosen a goal, it is important to be specific in order to make it a reality. It is also important to write down all the details. This is done by answering the questions: What? Why?

"What?" – Look at the goal you wrote down in Step 1. If you have a large goal such as "improving your life to the max," that is too broad. It is not specific enough to be able to take focused action.

The answer is to simplify it. How do you eat an elephant? Take one (small) bite at a time. It would be more productive to take "improving your life to the max" and break it down to a more manageable size.

Let's take my friend's goal for example. He wants to eventually quit smoking. A better statement would be "I am a non-smoker by (pick a date)." State the goal in the present tense.

Now answer "Why?" – Why do you want to do this? This is by far the most important question you need to answer. If you don't have a strong enough reason or a passion for what you are doing, then each time you set a goal, you will fail to see it through to the end. Is it a goal worth investing your time, money, energy, and other resources in?

"Why?" is the reason or passion behind your getting this result? If your "Why?" is strong enough, and focused enough, your goals will become a reality. They may not happen in the way that you are expecting or hoping that they will show up, because God may have other plans that will be even better for you in the long run.

If you are clear on your "Why?" you will overcome any challenges or obstacles that appear in your path to reach your desired goal. List at least three benefits that you will receive from reaching your goal. For instance, in the case of my friend who wants to stop smoking, the reasons "Why?" could be:

- I will have more money to spend on other things, like my daughter.

- I will be a better role model not only for my daughter, but I could become a speaker on this subject, and help others overcome their individual challenges through my example as a role model.

- I will lessen my chances of dying of lung cancer and leaving my daughter, or not being able to see my grandchildren.

If your "Why?" does not feel strong, or if it doesn't create a sense of urgency in you, then go back to Step 1 and choose a different goal.

Step 4: M = Measurable

In order to measure something, you must know the point of origin. In my friend's case, the question is: How many cigarettes per day is he currently smoking? Once he determines this, he can measure his progress by the number of cigarettes he does or doesn't smoke each day.

Next you will need ways of measuring your progress. For example, it could be things such as:

- Each day I smoke one less cigarette. - I attend three support-group meetings a week

- I use nicotine patches.

- I do not go to places where people are smoking.

- Whenever I feel like buying an extra pack of cigarettes, I will give that money to my daughter instead.

- When I feel like smoking extra, I will chew a stick of gum instead.
- I have an accountability partner.

Suppose you want to become a writer. If you want to write, what do you have to do? You have to write every day. Make it your goal to write 50 or 100 words, or 100 sentences a day, whatever seems feasible to you.

Step 5: A = Achievable

A goal must be achievable. It should be a challenge, something that will stretch you beyond what you normally do, but not so far out of reach that your subconscious mind keeps reminding you that it cannot be done.

For example, if you are in a wheelchair and you want to play basketball, is this achievable? Yes! There are wheelchair basketball teams.

Do not give up on your dreams. If your goal statement feels unachievable, then break it down to the first challenging, yet achievable, step in reaching the ultimate goal and focus on that.

Step 6: R = Realistic

Going back to the wheelchair basketball example, is it realistic that you will become a four-star player? Are you skilled enough and dedicated enough? It should also be a bit out of your comfort zone, but realistic. You know the saying, 'Know thy self'.

You also have to have enough knowledge about the subject to judge what is realistic, and you may need to consult with an expert. For example, I am not knowledgeable on certain financial matters. Therefore, I use a financial advisor, because he's been trained in it. What you don't know can hurt you.

If your goal statement is not realistic, then adjust it until it is.

Step 7: T = Timely

Pick a date by which your goal will be finalized. It is also a good idea to put milestone dates at intervals leading up to the final goal.

Step 8: GOALS

G = Greatness

Is your goal worthy of greatness? If it's minimal, it won't empower you to be able to do anything. It has to be something that excites you. That's why the 'why?' of it, is the most important part.

O = Open minded

Keep an open-mind; flexibility is key to the greatness of your goal. Be aware of other possibilities when they come along, and accept the fact that adjustments may need to be made along the way.

A = Attitude

Maintain a positive attitude in everything you do, and you will enjoy every step of the journey.

L = Learning

Be willing to learn new ways to improve on your goals. No matter what your goal, there is a learning process involved to reach success.

Once you set a goal, create a baseline, a starting point, a jump point, which means you need to know where you are right now. Your goal could be to be a motivational speaker. For example, if you are not used to speaking in front of a group of people, that could be your starting point.

S = Success

Visualize successfully reaching your goal. If you want to write a book, you have to imagine your finished book sitting on the table in front of you. How many pages does it have? How many chapters do you see? What are the chapter titles?

Step 9: Have a mentor review your goal plan, and be accountable to your mentor.

It may become a challenge to sort out your individual goals. You may need help to do this.

People and circumstances will appear in your path, as challenges that can throw off even the best of plans. We may even lie to ourselves, which is to have counter intuitive thoughts about what we really want. Worse yet, we may give up when we get distracted or become unfocused.

This is why it is so important to have a mentor, a coach, or someone who can give you proper guidance and hold you accountable.

Review of Setting SMART Goals

Remember that the most important part of this message is "Why?" do you want to have a particular goal? The answer to "Why?" will be the catalyst that gets you through the challenging times that may occur. For example, suppose you want to lose weight. There could be many reasons, but it must be your own good faith goal, not someone else's, for true motivation. Goals must be specific. If you were to say, "I want to lose weight", that isn't a goal, it's a dream, or a longing that you have. That means that it isn't specific. How much weight do you want to lose? Again, it has to be measurable. Is it achievable and realistic? There are those who believe they are overweight, when they actually are not. They may have an eating disorder; so be sure that your goal, whatever it may be is realistic. Lastly, what is the time frame? By what date are you going to lose the weight?

Goal Achieving

Let's consider the concepts taught by Bob Proctor. Once you set a goal, you begin to use your Scooby eyes and ears and antennas, to focus on what you want to achieve. It is getting in touch with the universe, the force, God, or whatever name you choose. This means, 'letting go and letting God' help you to reach your goal.

If you set a goal, do not be concerned with where the money will come from. Bob Proctor's answer to the question of where it would come from was, "Wherever it is right now, is where it will come from." This makes perfect sense to me. Whenever I want to do something, I visualize what I want to happen, and the means to do it shows up. That is the power to create from our thoughts.

It is fundamental that your 'Why', your reason for wanting the goal, is significant. That means you have to be emotionally invested in it. Emotion and passion will carry you through. It's not enough to say, "I want to be a millionaire." Be clear on the reason 'why' you want to become a millionaire. Having a million dollars doesn't necessarily mean you crave money, but you have to be emotionally attached to your outcome to make it manifest.

As you can see, achieving your goal involves activating "the Law of Attraction". When you decide on a goal and are committed to it, you begin to activate this Law of Attraction, thereby bringing it to you. People will show up in your life to help you make your goals become a reality. For example, my lovely assistant, Marvelous Michele, showed up in my life when I was waiting in line at the Department of Motor Vehicles. Divine intervention put me in the right place at the right time to meet her. I didn't arrange it, nor plan it into my schedule that day. I also did not plan to meet Frank Gasiorowski, my coach. God brought him into my life. You have to surrender control to a higher power and then rely on your inner voice to guide you.

Bob Proctor suggests carrying a 'Goal Card' in your pocket, and touching it now and then. In this way, you put your attention on the goal, and this draws the energy to you to make it happen. The Goal Card should be written by hand. The energy in writing this goal causes thinking, which causes the image, and then attracts more positive energy.

Everything has energy. Writing out your goals allows you to become attached to them. What you feed grows, and what you starve dies. A vacuum cannot exist. This is why we need to have structure in our lives. Otherwise, we feed the wrong things. If we really want personal growth, we must learn to be uncomfortable, that is, to step outside our comfort zone. Sometimes, getting out of that comfort zone can be a terrifying process. It means that fear (False Evidence Appearing Real), has crept into our consciousness. We simply have to get back into our heart space. Go back to finding your passion, and your passion will get you through it. Repetition is key here; you may have to go back there several times, until finally repetition makes you become comfortable with it. When you reach a certain level, like a peak, in which you encounter a barrier, you can always take it another step by going back to your passion, and repeating this until you are comfortable at the next level. In other words, repetition is the process by which we enlarge our comfort zone and reach a new level.

Visualization is key to making this manifest. Some people create vision boards. For example, John Assaraf, who was in the movie, "The Secret ©", tells a story about cutting out a picture of a house, and putting it on his vision board. Five years later, as he is unpacking in his new home, his son asks, "What is that?" and he replies, "It's a vision board". He pulls it out and the exact house, the exact property, that he had envisioned five years before, is the one he was now living in. That's how the Law of Attraction works.

It is important to focus on something. For me, I don't visualize it in terms of a picture; it's more of a feeling. When I am working with someone that I want to help, instead of visualizing them getting better, I feel them getting better. It is an emotional connection with that person, a feeling.

Be passionate about your goals. If you are doing this consistently, it will make all the difference in the world. I am passionate about helping other people. I want them to see what they consider to be their problems, as just challenges waiting to be changed into opportunities.

In summary, meeting a goal is a challenging, but rewarding process. In some cases, it will represent a major breakthrough in your life. There are different techniques that you can explore, such as SMART Goals, Vision Boards, and Goal Cards. Allow yourself to be directed by your passion, and use a mentor to give you an objective perspective.

Action Steps for Chapter Eight

Goal Setting and Goal Achieving

- What is your "Why?" for your biggest dreams? You must have a strong emotional attachment to getting the desired outcome.

- Examine your inner self to see if you are primarily visual (sight), auditory (hearing), sensory (feeling), or intuitive (knowing). Find out which senses are the strongest and use this knowledge for motivation.

- Go through the S.M.A.R.T. steps as outlined in this chapter.

- Make a vision board, of pictures that represent your goals.

- Make a small Goal Card, with your goal written on it. Carry it with you in your wallet to remind you at all times, and refer to it often.

- Expect miracles, and be prepared to seize the moment when an opportunity arises.

Chapter Nine

Distinctions and Decisions
are Keys to Success

By this time you may already be working on a goal, or at least have one in mind. Success in maximizing your happiness and reaching your goals is greatly impacted by the decisions you make along the way. The kind of decisions you make reflect your ability to make distinctions, which will support your goal.

Some key distinctions are knowing: if your heart and head are aligned; if there is a valid sense of urgency; what the long and short term impact of the decision will be for yourself and others; what other people's motives are; if you need to consult with an expert to get all the facts; and if the decision will move you towards your goal.

Whenever you are faced with needing to make an on-the-spot decision, which may involve a family member, or a friend, or a new acquaintance, there is at least one question you and I must ask ourselves, which is: Do your heart and your head agree that it is in your best interest to do what they are asking you to do right now?

Before I learned the value of asking this question, I made an on-the-spot decision in which my head and heart were not in agreement. This resulted in being taken advantage of by a person whom I've known for a while. I was so overjoyed to see her again, that I let my guard down, even though she had taken advantage of me in the past. I made the decision to do something for her before I was able to make the distinction of her motivation in seeking me out. I was not able to reconnect with my previous experiences with her. If I had given it more thought, I would have remembered that there had been a violation of my trust. I imagine that most people have had a similar occurrence in their lives, and can relate to this in one way or another.

One of my challenges is that my TBI (traumatic brain injury) inhibits my ability to make distinctions between my heart and my head. I am constantly learning to take a step back before making a decision. I recognize that people without disabilities also struggle with similar concerns. If you have a TBI, you have to be especially vigilant.

A sense of urgency can also affect your decision-making. Everyone's sense of urgency and importance differs from one person to the other. You have to be aware if you are taking action based on your own values and needs, or on someone else's.

For example, my former trustee wouldn't give me his phone number, because I considered everything urgent and important, which overwhelmed him. He realized that as time passed, many things became less urgent and less important. Some things would resolve themselves without taking action.

However, there was one challenge I had that was urgent and very important to me. I have a rental house on my property, and my tenant was without water for two weeks during the winter. We thought the water lines were frozen. I contacted that same trustee, and his solution was to wait until spring for her water to thaw out. I said, "That is unacceptable", so I hired a man who found the broken line and fixed it.

There was a difference between my perception of what was urgent and important, and what my trustee's prospective was. My heart knew there was a problem there, and my head said act on it. They were in 100% agreement. Other times, situations arise in which your head does not have enough knowledge. This happened to me when I bought some silver coins. They were supposedly found in the man's basement. I purchased them and took them to a local coin dealer. He said that they had all been dipped in a cleaning solution, which means they are only worth bullion value. I couldn't return them, because it had been over 30 days, and that was past their return policy. From my heart, I believed the man I bought them from, but my head had not received the full knowledge that they had been cleaned.

There are times when it does not occur to us that we could possibly be taken advantage of. It is kind of a blind trust that when we operate from a pure heart, we don't like to think that anyone would use for their own purposes without our knowledge or consent. When further information comes to light, we then realize we didn't do the right thing.

For example, my mother died in 1975, without a will. I suggested that my brother, uncle, and I divide up the property, and bid on certain things in the house. She had some old paintings drawn by a relative that at first glance, appeared to have little value. My uncle won the bid on those paintings. I found out many years later that my uncle had sold the paintings for a very large sum of money.

Because I didn't know what the value was at the time of making the bids, I went with my heart and my head. At the time, they were in 100% alignment; I did the best I could do. This means that you have to make yourself knowledgeable by gathering all the facts so that you can make and informed decision.

One area in which I feel that I am sufficiently informed is in my knowledge of comic books. For example, when a comic book collector is considering the purchase of any "rare" or older comic book, they must know the physical condition of it before deciding if it's a worthwhile purchase or investment. They then must look for the CGC grade and have the awareness to know that when buying a comic book there are often multiple copies of the same book with different grades on them. A higher grade is in better condition, with 10 being the highest, meaning that a 10 is worth much more in resale value than say, a 9 or an 8, or some lower grade. When comparing two issues of the same comic, a novice collector might presume that the one with the higher grade has the higher monetary or resale value. The more experienced and better informed collector, would know this may not be the case because there may be some other distinctions that the novice may have either overlooked in haste, or not been aware of at all.

For example, let's say you wanted to add Fantastic Four #1 to your collection, and were comparing two graded copies. The first, graded 8.0 out of 10, is a very fine comic, and is being offered to you way below the market value, lets say between $500 and $700. The second, rated lower at 7.5, is being offered to you for four times more, at $2,500.

A novice may make the mistake of thinking that they have gotten a great deal, and buys the higher graded comic book; only to be disappointed when he tries to sell it later, and discovers the actual facts. In reality, this copy is a reproduction and he has passed up purchasing the other one, or lower grade, which turned out to be an original copy worth more, even though it may have been altered or repaired. If the original was graded 8.0, and had not been restored it would be worth about $25,000. This is how one must use their discernment and knowledge, so as not be taken advantage of. Grading is, however, only one factor to be considered.

In critical moments we are often tested. Whenever I fail to have my heart and head in alignment, I end up making a bad decision. It makes me stronger and more aware of this process, for the next time I am tested. All that we can hope to do is to learn and grow from our past experiences.

There is something I want to mention for those with a traumatic brain injury (TBI) who have been assigned staff to help them. Whenever a person abuses you, takes advantage of you, steals from you, or anytime something is done outside what the system requires of you, your aides will have to file an incident report. There was a person who took advantage of me by asking me to give them a loan of a large sum of money, and in good faith, I did. This person used to be part of my staff, but wasn't at the time of the incident. I mentioned this had happened to either a current staff person or my therapist, and as soon as I did, they filed an incident report. Those whose job it was to protect me became very aware of how events unfolded. I had to actually file a police report against this person.

In order to be in TBI Waiver program, you are required to sign a document stating that you will not do anything illegal. That means that according to the laws of the state you live in, and any Federal laws that apply, you will not do anything that is illegal by their definition. For example, fraud, stealing, hiring a prostitute, or doing drugs, are some of the things that can cause you to lose your benefits.

You already know when you are breaking a law. However, what you may not realize is that if you contribute to someone else breaking the law, you may also be held accountable. For example, if you give money to someone, and they use it for illegal purposes, you could be considered an accessory to the crime, resulting in you losing your benefits of the waiver program. Additionally, you may not remember the system-specific guidelines which, when violated, would cause you to lose your services. Therefore, be aware that when you sign these documents, they are legally binding contracts. You can lose your program benefits if you do not abide by them.

This is all part of making distinctions and decisions. We constantly make decisions, and thereby, are constantly challenged in our determination to reach a goal. To make clear and strong distinctions and decisions, it is helpful to have a clear goal based on a passion, which is the underlying driver of your life.

The more you develop the ability to make key distinctions, the quicker you will be able to make confident decisions which support your success. The key distinctions covered in this chapter are knowing: if your heart and head are aligned; if there is a valid sense of urgency; what the long and short term impact of the decision will be for yourself and others; and what other people's motives are. You may need to consult with an expert to get all the facts before making your choices.

Action Steps for Chapter Nine

Distinctions and Decisions are Keys to Success

- Have you ever made a choice in which your heart and head were not in agreement? What was the choice? What was the result? Write this down.

- To build awareness, every day pick something you need to make a decision about. For example, something as simple as what to eat for lunch, or as complex as what career to follow. Close your eyes and breathe deeply, considering this question for a few minutes. Then, write down (1) what your heart feels, and (2) what your head thinks. If they are not aligned, keep doing this every day until you get clarity.

- Pick one issue/decision you have been wrestling with for a long time. Write it down. Then, write out your answers to these questions:

  1. What does your heart feel?

  2. What does your head say?

  3. Consider how other people will be affected by your decisions. How will they benefit if you do not change? And if you do change?

  4. What are the long-term effects of your decision?

  5. What are the short-term outcomes?

  6. Visualize this getting better in the future.

  7. Be the instrument of change and take the necessary required action.

Chapter Ten

Mentoring is the Fastest
Way to Success

Using a mentor has been suggested throughout this book. A good mentor is so important that I am dedicating a chapter to this topic. Every successful person has had some kind of mentor, and usually a network of mentors. An effective mentor can help you achieve success much faster than what you can do on your own, provided you take an active role with their guidance.

Following a mentor's advice does not mean childishly doing whatever someone tells you to do. It is critical to use your Scooby Ears and Eyes, which you have been developing, to find the right mentor for a particular objective, one who deserves your confidence and trust. Just as your mentor will be testing you, you should test your mentor.

Here is a paraphrase of an online definition of mentoring:

> Mentoring is a structured and trusting relationship that brings people together with caring individuals who offer guidance, support and encouragement aimed at developing the competence and character of the mentee.

My definition of a mentor is:

> A mentor is a wise man or woman who serves as a trusted counselor, teacher, and guide; someone who challenges

you to think, who inspires you to take action, and who holds you accountable for reaching your goals.

They are usually considered "elders" or are older because with age comes wisdom, but that may not be always true. There are some people who are born with great gifts that we refer to as natural talents. Many become aware of them at an early age, like Jesus. In more modern times, Michael Jordan is such an example. They all have had mentors. Jesus had God his Father; Michael Jordan had his coach, John Wooden. No one does it alone, and you need a network of people to help, if you want to be successful.

You have to use your Scooby Ears and Eyes to find good mentors. If you are working on goals, go back and review your goals and see if you are using your Scooby Ears and Eyes to assist you in bringing the right people into your life to help you reach your goals. If you are not finding the right people to help you, then ask your service coordinator for help, if you have one.

Aside from the people who are paid to guide you or assist you, mentors can be found almost anywhere. They can be family, friends, peers, acquaintances; they can be younger or older than you, male or female, and of different ethnic backgrounds. One necessary criterion for a good mentor is that they inspire you personally, professionally, or in whatever your specific goals are in life. Many people with TBI have paid staff that fill the mentor role to some extent, but it can't just be limited to these people if you want to grow as a person.

Seek out a mentor and see if they are the right fit for your needs. You may have to go through several mentors to find the one that works best for you. The search can have many frustrations, dead ends, and disappointments, or you may find a good mentor very easily; however, persistence is very important. Don't give up; the rewards far outweigh the disappointments. Make a list of people you can reach out to. Have backups so that if someone is not available at a time of urgent need, there is someone else you can contact. It's like having a Plan B.

If you have bigger goals, like becoming a published writer, or a speaker like me, then you may have to do some more searching. My coach, Frank Gasiorowski, Mr. 90-Day Goals, has been instrumental in my being a speaker, and now in publishing this book. He coaches me on a regular basis, and teaches me about things such as the overall process of publishing a book. He keeps me focused on the next step along the way.

Once you have selected a mentor whom you trust, you have to follow through and do what the mentor says. There are many different resources available, including people programs, and various motivational books. Many work, but few people follow them; they go from one thing to the next thing. It could be Tony Robbins this month, and then Marianne Williamson the next. That's because when people find a mentor they often do not do what the mentor is teaching.

If your mentor suggests doing something, and your heart and head are not in alignment with it, then discuss this with the mentor before proceeding. You are still responsible for your own actions and the results of those actions both on yourself and others that are impacted by them.

A mentor is a guide, but you still have to do the work yourself, of achieving your goals, which means you have to be disciplined. If I don't do everything my coach says, every week he has to repeat, "I can't beat you over the head." He doesn't physically beat me over the head, but we have to review what I've done, and there are certain things I have to do every day. Thank God I have this mentor; otherwise, this book would not have come into existence.

If you want to make a huge leap forward in your life, in the quickest amount of time, the smartest thing you can do is get a mentor. Not every mentor has the same expertise. Find one who is an expert in that specific area you want to make major improvements in, such as a health and/or nutrition coach, an internet marketing coach, a personal finance coach, etc. Use those Scooby ears to find the person who can best help you to achieve what you desire. If you role model the right person, or a company, you will reach your goal quicker.

In summary, using a mentor effectively can help you break through barriers that you were not able to get through on your own. They help you see those things that you were not aware of. They can advise you on the best course of action, because they have been there before. Use your Scooby Ears and Eyes to select appropriate mentors, and develop your relationship with them by following their instructions to the degree that it is in alignment with your passion and goals.

Action Steps for Chapter Ten

Mentoring is the Fastest Way to Success

- Do you already have a mentor? Do you have more than one? How can you make better use of this relationship?

- Make a list of people you can call when in need of help. Include their contact information (phone number, email, address, website, etc.) Carry this list with you for times when you have an inspired idea, or are in a crisis, or need some guidance. This is the beginning of your mentoring network.

- Start noticing people in your life, and find those whom you would like to be your mentor for a specific purpose. Approach that person and ask them to be your mentor. Make a commitment that you are going to follow their advice, as it aligns to both the mind and heart.

- Build a network of mentors. Have different mentors for different areas of your life.

Chapter Eleven

CANI-ing
(Consistent And Never-ending Improvement)

This last chapter represents a continuation, rather than an ending or summary, to what was discussed in this book.

There is a phrase that has meant everything to me. It's called CANI-ing, 'Consistent And Never-ending Improvement'. "CANI" is an expression that is taught by motivational speaker, Tony Robbins, at an *Unleash the Power Within* event. However, Tony used the word "Constant". Because of the way my mind works, I prefer to use the word "Consistent". I also add the "-ing" to the end to make it a verb, because of how I perceive time. Do you understand the difference between the meaning of doing something 'constantly' and 'being consistent'? 'Constant' to me has a negative anchor and makes me feel like I 'have to' continually do something. Does it for you? 'Consistent' to me has a positive anchor. 'Consistent' feels more self-directed, that way we take charge or take personal responsibility for ourselves. They may have only a slight difference in meaning to you, so chose the one that meets your needs and go with it.

There are only a couple of things in this world that are constant, which do not change. For instance, there are certain mathematical expressions, like the value "pi". If you believe in the Bible, God's love for you never changes. Those are just two examples of constant things.

However, we are all faced with other things that are always changing. We are aging; our bodies change with time. Our relationships are changing, be they of friends, business, aides, or family. The economy is changing, as are your own personal finances. Are you resistant to change, or do you embrace it?

CANI-ing means to take an idea or a project and be consistently improving or upgrading it. This expression is important to me because I have to change in order to grow. If you aren't changing, you are going to be left behind.

"Consistent and never-ending" includes doing something daily. I do consistent and never-ending inspired action every day. Whenever you have a problem, whether it is a relationship, financial, or even aging, you have to re-look at this using "CANI-ing."

Does the term 'daily', or 'in the moment', make you uncomfortable or excited? Does it feel too overwhelming to even consider? You have to decide how badly you want to improve your situation, and what level of discomfort you can tolerate to get there. In order to manifest any kind of change in order to grow, you have to step outside of your comfort zone and stretch to get there.

Take consistent and inspired action all the time. For example, my body is getting older, so I exercise five days a week at the YMCA for two hours, and have a goal to eat healthier. Every day I work on self-development, physically, mentally, emotionally and spiritually.

Relationships also take work; you know that you have to be consistently doing something to give each person in your life part of yourself.

The economy is what it is, but that means that everyone has their own personal economy. That means you have to budget your money and you have to know where your resources go.

Once you achieve a goal, such as losing weight by a target date, don't stop there. Go to the next level, of consistently keeping it off, and of improving other aspects of your life.

I also want to encourage everybody with a TBI who is in the system to be more proactive with the use of resources. You have aides; utilize their talents. I consistently seek to improve my staff. I'm always on the lookout for the best staff, and to utilize them in the best way I can.

Action Steps for Chapter Eleven

CANI-ing (Consistent And Never-ending Improvement)

- Think of a way you have naturally used CANI-ing in the past. What was the result?

- Notice your pattern when you try to do something new – do you take two steps forward and one step back? What makes you pick yourself up and try again? Or do you give up?

- Review the Goals chapter and reevaluate your goals. If the goal is strong but there are no results, then consider how to be more consistent in your values and actions. Is your "Why" strong enough? Get in touch with your "Why" and use this to propel you forward to be more consistent.

- Make a chart, to track your new behavior, or to track progress on a project/goal you are working on. Fill it in daily. If you need help taking a different action, report to a friend or accountability partner daily on how you've done. My sincere hope is that you have benefited from this book. I encourage you to proceed, 'CANI-ing' your life, by taking inspired action every day. May your life be full of passion, blessings, and ultimately, happiness.

Chapter Highlights

1. Disability: A Curse or a Gift from God?

What do you have that feels like a curse? Even people who are 'happy' may have something that feels like a dark cloud hanging over them.

Go ahead and allow yourself to feel yours. Is it something physical, a difficult relationship, no money, or the death of a loved one?

How would you like to change this? I felt cursed with being "disabled" the rest of my life. I now see that I am 'Blessed'! How did the very thing that cursed me become my blessing? My perspective changed; how about yours? What are you focusing on?

2. How I Turned my 'Disability' into an Asset

An asset is defined as something that gives you cash flow.

Whatever kind of "disability" you may have, find out what federal/state/local programs you can apply for.

When thought of in terms of money, these services are an asset because someone else is paying money for them.

You will find that there are a variety of services that these agencies can provide, that you may have never considered.

An important point is to see every person who comes to your house as if they are a blessing. They are there to help you.

3. From Problems to Challenges to Opportunity

Say "problem" aloud ten times - how do you feel? Say "opportunity" aloud ten times - how do you feel?

When I say "problem" it feels like there is no solution. It is heavy, depressing, dark. When I say "opportunity" it feels exciting. It is full of possibility, growth, and light.

For every "problem", think outside the box. Suspend your limiting belief that there is no solution. You have to go to your spirit, your heart. You have to say, "There has to be something I am not seeing here." Realizing that you have other choices, your 'problems' will become 'challenges'. These 'challenges' move into 'opportunities'.

4. Scooby Ears and Eyes

"Scooby Ears and Eyes" is named after the cartoon "Scooby Doo Where Are You?" It is a metaphor for your Reticular Activating System (RAS), which is part of your brain.

Scooby Doo is a dog whose ears shot up and head turned, whenever he sensed danger or something else that needed to be paid attention to so that a spooky mystery could be solved.

This illustrates how your RAS works. Every minute we have a million different impulses that go into our brain. Your RAS, or your Scooby Ears and Eyes, sort what is important to you.

Remember, we get what we focus on.

5. Using Adversity to Discover Hidden Talents

I believe that everyone has a hidden talent.

How do you discover your talent if it is hidden? This comes through adversities, which are tests; and life is full of them! When a life-changing event occurs, there are always tests. Even happy events, such as falling in love, have big tests attached to them.

When you face a difficult test, you find yourself having to do something that you never did before, and that you didn't even think that you could do. It is at these times that hidden talents rise to the occasion and you are able to do something naturally that you did not know you could.

6. Fantastic Frank Is My Brand

"Branding" is something powerful that you can do to re-enforce the changes you make as you recognize blessings, see opportunities, and develop hidden talents.

A "brand" is something that other people recognize and remember. Like Coca Cola: "Coke, The Real Thing" - that's a brand. Our minds and bodies are affected by words. You may not realize it, but you are already branding yourself with words that you use to describe yourself. If I live my life as "Disabled Frank", that means I am disabled.

When I live as "Fantastic Frank", I am better defined. I encourage you to find your brand and have fun with it!

7. Move from Depression to an Improved State of Mind

The words that you use have 'anchors' which trigger a particular emotional state, positive or negative.

If you use the words "depressed" to describe yourself you will be reinforcing that state, and it will become your identity.

That's why I never say that I am depressed. Happiness can be improved dramatically by using words that shift you from a negative state to a positive one.

For example, instead of referring to myself as being "disabled", I say that I am "differently-abled".

It is also important to surround yourself with positive people, a positive environment, and to minimize time focusing on negative subjects.

8. Goal Setting and Goal Achieving

There are many different reasons to set goals.

One that I like is:

To achieve or to maximize the sense of wellness in any area of our lives, we need to set goals.

As you get in touch with your passion, something specific that you want to achieve will begin to take shape.

When this occurs, it is time to set a goal.There are two aspects to making your Goals manifest.

One is Goal "Setting" and the other is Goal "Achieving". Most importantly, be sure you have a big enough reason, as to "Why" you are setting a goal.

9. Distinctions and Decisions are Keys to Success

Maximizing your happiness and reaching your goals is greatly impacted by the decisions you make along the way.

Whenever you are faced with needing to make a decision, we must ask ourselves:

Does my heart and my head both agree with this decision? If other people are involved, what are their motives? Do I need to consult with an expert to get all the facts? Will making this decision move me towards my goal?

The more you develop the ability to make key distinctions, the quicker you will be able to make confident decisions which support your success.

10. Mentoring is the Fastest Way to Success

Every successful person has had some kind of mentor and usually a network of mentors for different areas of their life. An effective mentor, rightly used, can help you achieve success much faster than what you can do on your own.

A mentor is a guide, but you still have to do the work yourself. You are still responsible for your own action and the impact of those actions.

Just as your mentor will be testing you, you should test your mentor. One necessary criterion for a good mentor is that they inspire you personally, professionally, or in whatever your specific goals in life are.

11. CANI-ing (Consistent And Never-ending Improvement)

There is a phrase that has meant everything to me. It's called CANI-ing, Consistent And Never-ending Improvement. CANI- ing means to take an idea or a project and consistently upgrade it.

Once you achieve a goal, such as losing weight by a target date, don't stop there. Go to the next level, of consistently keeping it off, and of improving other aspects of your health.

You have to find out how badly you want to improve your situation, and what level of discomfort you can tolerate to get there. In order to manifest any kind of change to grow, you have to step outside of your comfort zone.

RESOURCES

John Assaraf – The Spiritual Entrepreneur
   http://www.johnassaraf.com

Joel Bauer – Passion 2 Profit
   http://joelbauer.com/

Michael Chapple – Home Fire Safety
   http://www.homefiresafety.com

Dr. Mike Davison – Coach
   http://www.partnersinpurpose.com/

Dr. Wayne Dwyer – Motivational Author
   http://www.drwaynedyer.com/

T. Harv Eker - Money Expert
   http://www.millionairemindevents.com

Doug Evans - Coach
   http://discoveryourmissingpower.com/

Frank Gasiorowski – Mr. 90DayGoals
   http://www.90daygoals.com/

Mike Litman – "You don't have to get it right, you just have to get it going."
   http://www.mikelitman.com/

James Malinchak – Motivational Speaker
   http://malinchak.com/

Stephen Pierce – Internet Marketing Consultant
   http://www.stephenpierceinc.com/

Tracy Repchuk – Internet Marketing & Social Media Strategist
   http://tracyrepchuk.com/

Anthony Robbins – Motivational Speaker and Life Coach
   http://www.tonyrobbins.com/

Justin Sachs – Justin Sachs Companies, including Motivational Press
   http://justinsachscompanies.com/

Max Simon – Big Vision Business
   http://bigvisionbusiness.com/

Stephen Simon – Film Producer
http://spiritualcinemacircle.com/

Nick Vujicic – "No arms, No legs, No worries!"
http://www.lifewithoutlimbs.org/

Neal Donald Walsch – Author
http://www.nealedonaldwalsch.com/

For More on Fantastic Frank Johnson

Website: www.FantasticFrankJohnson.com

To Book Fantastic Frank as a Speaker for your Convention,
Radio Show, or TV Segment
Call (585) 625-1820
Email Frank@FantasticFrankJohnson.com

About the Author

Fantastic Frank, born Frank R. Johnson, is the epitome of perseverance. As a young man, he was a successful chemical engineer and entrepreneur. One day while he was at the height of enjoying success, he was trapped in a fire, brought out in a body bag, and his life changed forever. As a result, he incurred a Traumatic Brain Injury (TBI). It was necessary for him to re-learn everything; including how to walk and talk. Now he is motivated to inspire millions.

Every day Frank meets his challenges, and is fueled with a passion to help others with his engaging, creative manner which is awe inspiring to everyone he meets.

Some of Fantastic Frank's significant accomplishments consist of publishing a comic book, "The Young Explorers ©" and as a motivational speaker, he captivates and touches audiences like no other. Frank is an internationally published author and the host of two BlogTalkRadio shows and he will show you how to overcome ANY obstacle.

Frank touches many people's lives daily - let him touch yours.

How Would You Like a FREE Special Bonus?

Thank you for purchasing this book, and allowing me the privilege of being your motivation for inspiration. For *more* Motivational Secrets, get instant access to a Free Guide by going to http://turndisabilitytoability.com/

CPSIA information can be obtained at www.ICGtesting.com
Printed in the USA
BVOW03s0540180913

331433BV00003B/8/P